Ireland:
Republicanism and Revolution

(The revolutionary dialectic of Republicanism)

By Alan Woods

Preface by Gerry Ruddy

Ireland: Republicanism and Revolution
By Alan Woods

First published by Wellred May 2005
Preface by Gerry Ruddy
Copyright © Wellred Publications

UK distribution: Wellred Books, PO Box 50525
London E14 6WG, England
Tel: +44 (0) 207 515 7675
Email: appeal@socialist.net

USA distribution: Wellred Books, PO Box 1331
Fargo, ND, 58103, USA.

Wellred on-line bookshop sales:
wellred.marxist.com and wellredusa.com

Typeset by Wellred
Printed by intypelibra, London, England

British Library Cataloguing in Publication Data
A catalogue record for this book is available from the British Library

ISBN: 1 9000 07 20 7

Cover design by Espe Espigares

Dedication

I dedicate this book to the memory of that great revolutionary Marxist and martyr of the working class, James Connolly.

Preface

Irish Republicanism is in crisis and not for the first time. Generation after generation of Irish Republicans have thrown themselves into the struggle against the British occupation of Ireland. Some of the finest flower of their generation fell in death and defeat in the struggle. One only has to mention, among others in a long litany of dead, the names Tone, Emmet, Connolly, Mellows, McCann, Costello, Bunting and Power[1] to realise that indeed the best and most radical people of every generation had flocked to the banners of Republicanism. And yet each generation fought and failed.

It is customary to learn from experience and indeed the best elements learn from the defeats of the previous generations. James Connolly was unrelenting in his criticism of the nationalists of his day, having analysed Irish history and quite correctly saw that militant nationalism even when it masqueraded as Republicanism would be unable to deliver full freedom from the British Empire. His writings were so dangerous to the aspirations of the Irish capitalist class that for nearly a full fifty years James Connolly, Marxist Republican socialist, was presented to the Irish people as a good Irish Catholic nationalist.

Liam Mellows, when the armed Republicans split over the Treaty, quickly realised it was a class struggle between Empire or the Republic and they, the Republicans, had to take up the class questions if they were to succeed. To justify his execution, the Free Staters were quick to release his writings and brand them communist in a country overwhelming under the rule of the crozier of the Roman Catholic Church. This was a McCarthyite witch-hunt before anyone had heard of Senator Joe McCarthy.

When the IRA under the influence of radical socialist and communist ideas declared a new political party called Saor Eire, the Roman Catholic Church once more raised its voice and the IRA leadership fell into line. During the Thirties the Roman Catholic Church was to the forefront in attacks against the radical left. It was sufficient to call organisations or individuals communist to weaken their influence.

During the Nineteen Fifties while the unemployed of Dublin were electing two of their number to the Dail on the back of unemployment protests, Republicans were planning Operation Harvest[2] and were told to ignore social and economic issues. The failure of Operation Harvest led to a rethink.

Seamus Costello, who had been involved in the armed campaign, was in the forefront of the swing to the left. With the emergence of the Civil Rights struggle the Republican left was in the ascendancy but with the outbreak of violence the Free Staters with guns and money split the Republican movement and backed the emergent anti-communist Provisional Republican movement. The subsequent decision by the Official Republican movement to back the concept of the reform of the Six-County state led to Seamus Costello and other comrades walking away to form a party based around the most advanced ideas of republican socialism. That party was the Irish Republican Socialist Party, a party I have the privilege of being a member of.

The ideas of Republican Socialism have been so dangerous to the powers that be that they encouraged armed attacks on our Party to wipe us out. In the Nineteen Seventies, Eighties and Nineties, armed attacks were launched against our movement leading to the tragic loss of great thinkers and charismatic leaders like Seamus Costello, Ta Power and Gino Gallagher. During all this time our movement made many mistakes. But we have learned from those mistakes. The greatest weapon we have is our ideas. And it was our ideas that lead us to correctly analyse the Good Friday Agreement. We called for a "no vote", arguing it would institutionalise sectarianism, fall far short of Republican aspirations and copper fasten partition. Our own analysis, we were glad to find, was shared by the author of this book.

Alan Woods has here written a book that will make uncomfortable reading for many Republicans. It is a trenchant criticism of Republicanism based on a Marxist analysis. One does not have to share Alan's perspectives however to see great validity in much of what he says. Hopefully, it will stimulate debate and analysis. Serious revolutionaries, genuine Marxists, committed Republicans will read this book with thoughtful interest. They will give it the respect it deserves. Of course many others on the left will reject his perspectives and indulge in the usual leftist rhetoric that passes for political criticism. Alan's past membership of the Militant tendency in Britain will be enough for those who play at politics to write his ideas off without taking the trouble to read them. People of a narrow nationalist outlook will ask what gives him, a Brit, the right to comment on Irish Republicanism. These same people forget that James Connolly was from Scotland, Erskine Childers was an Englishman and Eamon De Valera, a citizen of the U.S.A. Where people come from matters not today.

In a world of rampant imperialism it is clear that nationalism has little or nothing to offer. On the other hand, here in Ireland a radical Republicanism based on the centrality of the working class to its own liberation and the most advanced ideas of the working-class movement worldwide has a lot to offer the working class. That Republicanism must not be confused with those who pander to nationalism and tried to build a pan nationalist front with the enemies of the working class.

That Provo Project has failed. Despite acts of decommissioning, despite paying homage to the war-mongering George Bush and accepting the restoration of Stormont and making some electoral gains by donning the clothes of Fianna Fail and the SDLP, Sinn Féin Provisionals have seen their elected Assembly closed down four times and their strategy based on the Good Friday Agreement collapse.

Now is the time for a rethink for all those who genuinely have an anti-imperialist and socialist perspective. Hopefully this book will stimulate a new debate for Irish Republicanism. A new turn is necessary. Armed struggle is no longer a viable option and the Republican dream of uniting "Catholic, Protestant and Dissenter" seems pie in the sky when we see the rising levels of sectarianism in working-class districts.

When the members of the Republican Socialist Movement took back control of that movement from an apolitical leadership in 1994/5, they were guided by the writings in particular of Ta Power because he had so much to say about the internal mechanisms within revolutionary organisations. Based on those writings, we have in the RSM returned to our roots of Republican socialism.

We firmly believe that if this book by Alan Woods begins a process by which Republicans and socialists return to Connolly and the best ideas of the Irish and international left, then the future struggle for socialism in Ireland will be greatly advanced.

Gerry Ruddy (Ard-Comhairle member, Irish Republican Socialist Party)
Belfast, 1st March 2005

---

[1] Wolfe Tone, father of Irish republicanism, died 1798; Robert Emmet died after abortive uprising in Dublin 1803; James Connolly, outstanding figure of Irish socialism and Marxism and executed fro his part in 1916 uprising; Liam Mellows, radical republican executed by Free Staters 1922; Joe Mc Cann, left wing socialist member of the official IRA gunned down by British Army 1972; Seamus Costello, Ronnie Bunting, Ta Power founding members of the Republican Socialist movement, all murdered by the enemies of the Irish working class.

[2] Operation Harvest was the name of the IRA operation against the Six-County state 1956-61. It was a dismal failure.

Foreword

We live at a turning point in world history. It is a time in which many idols have fallen, and in which men and women all over the world are thinking hard about which direction to take. For many it seems that the harsh sacrifices made in the course of a lifetime of struggle has been in vain. The old systems of oppression remain in place, seemingly set in stone. They seem to laugh at our efforts to overthrow them. They say to us: *"Miserable fools that you are!" Did you really believe you could ever succeed?"*

Ours is an age when once cherished ideals are trampled brutally underfoot. It is the age of the cynic, the opportunist, the careerist and the turncoat, of people who permit themselves the luxury of spitting on their own past and encouraging the young people to become like themselves: pitiful creatures with no belief in the past, no life in the present and no hope in the future. Deprived of its ideals, the young generation is being suffocated like a man slowly drowning in a fetid bog.

We have known such periods before: periods of apostasy that always follow hard on the heels of a great historic defeat. They seem never ending, like a dark night that never dawns. But just as the night always gives way to the day, such periods end in new and even greater upheavals. The human spirit cannot remain forever submerged in the Slough of Despond. Beneath the surface of apparent calm and stagnation new forces are being prepared, new contradictions engendered. Sooner or later they will burst to the surface.

I am old enough to remember the period of the 1950s and '60s, which also seemed stagnant and never-ending. But I also remember the tremendous revolutionary upheavals in France in 1968, which I experienced first hand. I remember how the supposedly apolitical and cynical youth took to the streets of Paris and fought bare handed against the armed thugs of the CRS. I remember too how this worldwide revolt of the youth found its reflection in Ireland with the Civil Rights movement in the Six Counties, when courageous young men and women faced the wrath of the B-Specials and the Paisleyite thugs.

That movement was an inspiration to us all. I am a Welshman by birth and a proletarian internationalist by conviction. I do not believe in frontiers of any kind because I believe that the nation state has outlived its usefulness and that it is the task of the working class to sweep away all frontiers. But as a Marxist I am duty bound to support every struggle against oppression, whether social or national.

I was a young student in 1968-9, following with passionate interest the dramatic events unfolding in the Six Counties. I did not see these events as something alien to myself. To my way of thinking, the struggles of the youth in Derry and Belfast was my struggle, their enemies my enemies, their cause my cause. How they fought! Yet ultimately their fight did not succeed. It did not fail for lack of courage. If there is one quality that the people of Ireland never lacked it is courage. But we are in a war, and in war courage by itself is never enough to win. How many times in the history of warfare has a big army composed of brave soldiers been defeated by a smaller force of well-trained professionals led by good generals?

They say a defeated army learns well. It would be a very poor outlook if that were not the case! After every defeat it is necessary to adopt that marvellous maxim of Spinoza: "Neither weep nor laugh – understand!" If we are prepared to ponder on the causes of defeat, to analyse them calmly and to draw the conclusions, then we can begin to pull things together again, regroup the old fighters and give them a perspective, win new recruits among the youth and educate them on the correct methods of fighting. We can prepare for the new battles that impend – for such battles are inevitable.

The first condition for a new beginning is to have the courage to face up to past mistakes, not to take refuge in false optimism, lies and self-deception. It is necessary to look the truth squarely in the face. It is necessary to say what is. That can be a painful experience but it is the only way in which one can put the past behind one and take a step forward.

The present work has doubtless many defects. It will have its fair share of critics and detractors, and many will strongly disagree with its central premises. That is not a problem. It is intended to provoke a debate on the central questions of the Irish Revolution. If it does not give all the answers, I hope that it at least has the merit of asking the questions that need to be asked. At a time when most of the Left in Britain and internationally seems to have nothing at all to say about Ireland, that seems to me to be at least something.

The last thing the present work claims to be is original. I do not say anything new here, but merely restate the traditional ideas of what we call Marxism and what I believe is known as Republican socialism in Ireland. Everything I have said and written was said and written long ago – and much better – by that great Marxist revolutionary and martyr of the working class, James Connolly. And when some people ask me why I still defend these "old" ideas, I answer simply: because we still have the "old" problems.

After the fall of the USSR many have written off Marxism as a force in the world and even as an idea. Like a baneful chorus in a Greek tragedy the enemies of socialism chant their tedious lines: the end of socialism the end of Marxism, the end of history. They work on the well-known principle of Josef Goebbels, Hitler's propaganda minister, that if a big lie is repeated often enough, people will begin to believe it.

Yet history has not ended and every day that passes we see that the capitalist system is in an ever-deeper crisis. There is no way forward for humanity on the basis of capitalism. And there is no future for the struggle for the national and social emancipation of the people of Ireland unless it is part of a struggle for the socialist transformation of society. The struggle against the old oppression in Ireland will triumph under the leadership of the working class or it will never triumph. That was the message of James Connolly, and it is the message of the present book. It has been vindicated time and time again in Irish history, and in the most tragic way in the history of the last thirty years. And just as an army needs officers in order to win a war, so the working class needs a party, a programme and a revolutionary leadership to overthrow the bourgeois state and take power into its hands.

The message of this book is that the destiny of Ireland is a Workers' Republic, a republic of those who Wolfe Tone called the men and women of no property, a free Republic without landlords, bankers and capitalists. It is a message of hope not despair, of confidence in the future of Ireland, the working class and socialism. It is a non-sectarian message equally addressed to all thinking people from different backgrounds, political convictions, religions and other opinions, but especially to the cadres and the youth of the Republican movement, who have paid a very heavy price for the last thirty years and who are now seeking explanations. If it helps even in the smallest way to get people to pause and think on the lessons of the past and the way forward, it will have been worthwhile.

My thanks to Espe Espigares for the design and layout of the book, to Rob Sewell for proof reading and Phil Mitchinson for his advice on different matters pertaining to Irish history and politics. I would also extend my appreciation to comrade Gerry Ruddy for his invaluable comments on the book when it was still in the manuscript stage and his incisive and helpful foreword. I would like to extend my particular thanks to my dear friend and comrade Peter Black, a veteran Irish socialist Republican who originally gave me the idea of this book and provided me with much invaluable documentary material for it.

Alan Woods, London, 4th March, 2005.

Introduction

The signing of the Good Friday Agreement and the subsequent ceasefire of the Provisional IRA after 30 years of armed struggle raises the question: after so much sacrifice and bloodshed, what has been achieved? Yet this question is being studiously avoided by the leaders of Sinn Féin, who have exchanged the armed struggle for a minister's portfolio. Though they publicly deny it, the unification of Ireland is off the agenda. The strategy, methods and tactics of non-socialist Republicanism have ended in complete disaster.

The Irish Republican movement has been struggling for a united Ireland for decades. Yet today it is clear to all that it is no nearer this objective than when it was founded.

Marxists have always been in favour of a united Ireland, but following in the footsteps of James Connolly, we have also understood that this goal can only be achieved as part of the struggle for a socialist Ireland and a socialist Britain. It can only be achieved by class and revolutionary methods. The prior condition is to unite the working class in struggle, and this can only be achieved by a return to the revolutionary traditions and programme of Jim Larkin and James Connolly - the programme of the *Workers' Republic*. So long as capitalism dominates Ireland there will be sectarian division and strife, which will undermine and destroy the movement for Irish unification.

It is particularly noteworthy that all those on the Left in Britain and internationally who for years were happy to act as cheerleaders for the Provisional IRA now have nothing to say on the subject. They have lapsed into an embarrassed silence, which reflects their complete lack of understanding of the "Irish question" and the extreme light-mindedness with which they habitually approach the national question, on which they have long ago abandoned the Marxist position and capitulated to bourgeois and petty bourgeois nationalism. This leads inevitably to one defeat and betrayal after another. And still they learn nothing!

He who does not learn from history will forever be doomed to repeat it. It is time to take stock of the past of the Republican movement and to draw a balance sheet. Only by such means can we extricate ourselves from the present impasse, and build the revolutionary movement urgently needed to prevent a further descent into sectarian chaos and achieve instead the historic task of overthrowing capitalism and constructing the 32-county Socialist Republic.

Part One

The national question and the class question

Josef Dietzgen once observed that when an old man considers his past life, he inevitably sees it as a long series of errors, and if he could live his life over again, he would doubtless prefer to eliminate these errors. But then he is left with the dialectical contradiction that it is only through these errors that he has arrived at wisdom. Everyone makes mistakes. There is no disgrace in that. But what is really unforgivable is to fail to learn from one's mistakes and profit by them. What is true for an individual is also true for the revolutionary party.

It is time to take stock of the past of the Republican movement and to draw a balance sheet. It is necessary to examine past mistakes and honestly admit them. It is necessary to call things by their right name. Only by such means can we avoid such mistakes in the future, and prepare the revolutionary forces that will eliminate capitalism and bring about the Irish Socialist Republic.

The national question can play a progressive or a reactionary role in history, depending on its class content. Marxists always ask the question: what class interests are served by a given movement, in order to determine our attitude to it. *Which class leads*? This is the decisive question. It has been the misfortune of the Irish national struggle ever since the death of James Connolly, that its leadership has fallen into the hands of the bourgeoisie and the petty bourgeoisie. This has determined both its character and the outcome.

It is necessary to cut through the fog of patriotic verbiage and rhetoric and lay bare the class interests that lie behind it. That was always the method of Connolly, who consistently approached the national question from a class standpoint. Only when we have done this will it be possible to separate what is progressive from what is reactionary in any given movement.

This is above all necessary when dealing with the national question, because here the bourgeoisie has a vested interest in concealing its real interests behind a smokescreen of mysticism and demagogy. Connolly always poured scorn over such mystification of the national question. He taught the working class to steer clear of the nationalist bourgeoisie - the enemies of labour. As for the petty bourgeois nationalists of Sinn Féin and the Irish Volunteers, he regarded them at best as unstable and unreliable allies in whom little trust could be placed. At most, it was sometimes necessary to reach temporary agreements for unity in action with the latter, but there could be no question of fusing with them. The first condition was: no programmatic blocs, no mixing up of banners: "March separately, and strike together!" Unfortunately, all this was forgotten after Connolly was killed following the Easter Rising.

Contradictions in the Republican movement

As in all things, there are contradictions within the Republican movement. This has always been true from the moment of its inception. The contradictions we are talking about ultimately have a class character. Whoever is not capable of seeing this will never be able to understand the history of the movement or what has happened to it. Neither will they be able to show a way forward out of the impasse in which the movement now finds itself.

There were always various elements within Irish Republicanism. We can divide these into two main strands since 1916. They can be seen in the differences between the Irish Citizen Army (ICA) and the Irish Volunteers. The revolutionary-proletarian tendency of the ICA attempted to hold on to its identity, but was thwarted by the reformist leadership of the labour movement that abandoned Connolly's class line after his death and capitulated to the bourgeois and middle class nationalists.

The latter, of course, have done everything in their power to bury the traditions of Connolly – the traditions of republican socialism. They have attempted – with some success – to force the Irish working class to subordinate its class interests to the alleged interests of the "national cause". They seek to blur the class lines and promote an imaginary unity of interest of all Irish people. This is a lie and a deception that has been disastrous alike for the cause of labour and the cause of Ireland, as Connolly correctly predicted.

Ever since 1916 there has been a struggle – either open or subterranean – between these two antagonistic trends. One wing of Republicanism is under the influence of bourgeois ideology. It constantly circumscribes the movement to the narrow confines of the capitalist system. It attempts to play down the existence of the class struggle and thus *in practice* subordinates the interests of the Irish workers to those of the Irish bourgeoisie. The fact that the people concerned sometimes pay lip service to socialism ("as the *final goal*") and the working class has no importance. In life and in politics, what counts is deeds, not words. The programme of the first Dail, heavily influenced by the ICA, was considered "Communistic" by the then IRA leadership. In the 1970s the hostility of the right-wingers in the Provisional IRA to socialism was such that they organised the burning of left-wing books.

From a theoretical standpoint, the right wing of Republicanism (up to the present, the dominant wing) stands on the "theory of stages": that is to say, the working class must forget about the struggle for socialism and concentrate everything on the fight to remove the Border. In the context of Ireland this idea - that once Ireland is re-united all our problems will somehow be solved, and then the question of socialism can be safely put back on the agenda as "the final goal", in maybe the next hundred years or so - was already discredited and exposed by Connolly over a century ago. Yet this theory is considered by its adherents as "realism", which indicates that at least they do not lack a sense of humour.

The cause of Ireland is the cause of labour and the cause of labour is the cause of Ireland and the two cannot be dissevered, as Connolly explained. Those who seek to artificially divide this intimately linked struggle for the liberation of Ireland and the creation of a 32-county Socialist Republic, do so in order to promote the importance of one over the other. The Official IRA, for example, argued that the social questions were more important than the national question. In reality, this was the cover behind which they hid their abandonment of the national liberation struggle in favour of reformism and respectability.

For the bourgeois and petit bourgeois nationalists meanwhile, it seems you can be in favour of socialism or not as you like as long as you postpone that struggle, subordinate it to the national question, which they seek to separate from the revolutionary struggle to transform Ireland.

Connolly wrote in the most uncompromising terms against such nationalism that expected the working class to struggle to gain new masters rather than their own liberty.

"The nationalism of men who desire to retain the present social system is not the fruit of a natural growth but is an ugly abortion, the abortive product of an attempt to create a rebellious movement in favour of political freedom among men contented to remain industrial slaves. It is an attempt to create a revolutionary movement towards freedom and to entrust the conduct of the movement to a class desirous of enforcing the social subjection of the men they are professing to lead… It professes to believe that the class grinding it down to industrial slavery can at the same moment be leading us forward to national liberty." (*The Workers Republic,* October, 1899.)

The argument that the working class must subordinate itself to the cause of Ireland, that we must set our class demands to one side and wait for a united Ireland to solve all our problems, was answered by Connolly long ago. He wrote:

"If you remove the English Army tomorrow and hoist the green flag over Dublin Castle, unless you set about the organisation of the Socialist Republic your efforts would be in vain.

"England would still rule you. She would rule you through her capitalists, through her landlords, through the whole array of commercial and individualist institutions she has planted in this country and watered with the tears of our mothers and the blood of our martyrs.

"England would rule you to your ruin, even while your lips offered hypocritical homage at the shrine of that Freedom whose cause you betrayed." (*Socialism and Nationalism*, January, 1897.)

How prophetic were these words! And how accurately they describe everything that happened in Ireland after 1916!

Another Tendency

But there has always been another tendency within Republicanism, the wing that stands close to the proletariat and strives to unite with the working class and the labour movement. Although it has traditionally lacked a clear grounding in theory, and has therefore lacked the necessary ideological weapons to fight against the bourgeois wing, this tendency has always existed and at times has gained ground at the expense of the right wing. Unfortunately, its lack of theory has led to inconsistencies and vacillations in the face of the right wing, which, though politically ignorant, has derived strength (and finance) from its proximity to the Southern capitalist class.

However, this other strand in the Republican movement continues to exist, though this fact has been ignored by the Left internationally. It is a condemnation of these "Lefts" that for 30 years, under the pretext of "supporting the Irish national liberation struggle", they uncritically backed the right wing Republicans of the Provisional IRA. Now that the latter has effectively thrown in the towel, their "left-wing" admirers in Britain and other countries have suddenly fallen silent. This is quite natural since they really have nothing interesting to say about Ireland – or anything else. We pass over these people with contempt, and address ourselves only to those honest Republicans who are now seriously examining the past and thinking about the future.

The great majority of the "Left" groups in Britain were reduced to the pathetic role of cheerleaders of Adams and McGuiness, therefore they had no interest in the left wing Republicans who attempted to take an independent line. The latter were systematically ignored and sidelined. The opening of fraternal dialogue between the Irish Republican socialists and the British Marxists would be beneficial to the working class movement of both countries. We must learn from each other, drawing on the rich experience of the class struggle in order to work out the correct perspectives, strategy and tactics for the struggle against capitalism and imperialism.

The Socialist Republicans, although a minority within the movement, have consistently striven to adopt a class line and a socialist perspective. For this reason they were deliberately targeted by the enemies of socialism: not only British imperialism and the secret services of the state, but also the right wing of the Republican movement. Many of the most advanced and conscious elements were assassinated. It is sufficient to mention the names of Seamus Costello and Ta Power in this regard.

The forces of British imperialism were well aware that ultimately their most dangerous enemies were not the gunmen and bombers but the political elements on the left wing of Republicanism. From the moment the British army set foot in the North, they set about trying to eliminate the "Communists", a concern that they shared with the Southern ruling class and its allies in the leadership of the Provisional IRA at that time.

However, all the repression in the world cannot destroy the revolutionary element in Republicanism, which manifests itself with redoubled force at every key turning point, including the present moment. The proletarian socialist tendency represented by James Connolly will always re-assert itself and challenge the hegemony of the bourgeois and petty bourgeois trend that has led the movement historically from one disaster to another.

At the present time Ireland stands once more at the crossroads, and with it the Republican movement. The strategy of so-called "armed struggle" that was pursued for three decades and for which a terrible price was paid, lies in ruins. The leadership of Provisional Sinn Féin has reached a deal with British imperialism – a deal in which the goal of a 32-county Republic does not feature. In reality the Good Friday Agreement and the institutions that have flowed from it are a sham and a deception. They represent a cruel trap with which to ensnare the desire of the majority of the population for peace. As such, despite its understandably gaining a majority in the referendum, the Marxists and the Republican socialists alike opposed it, and told the truth, no matter how unpalatable, to the working class of Ireland and Britain.

The legacy of bitterness and distrust left behind by "the Troubles" has deepened the divisions between the two communities in the North to unprecedented levels. The power of British imperialism has not even been dented. In fact, after all this effort and sacrifice, Irish unity is now further away than at any time in history.

It is time to draw a balance-sheet of the history of the national liberation struggle in Ireland and draw the necessary conclusions – for he who does not learn from history will always be doomed to repeat it.

The whole history of the last 100 years proves that the bourgeoisie is completely incapable of carrying through any of its historical tasks. They have completely confirmed the analysis of James Connolly in this regard. Even in the epoch of the bourgeois-democratic revolution in Europe, Marx and Engels mercilessly unmasked the cowardly, counterrevolutionary role of the bourgeoisie, and emphasised the need for the workers to maintain a policy of complete class independence, not only from the bourgeois liberals, but also from the vacillating petty bourgeois democrats:

"The proletarian, or really revolutionary party," wrote Engels, "succeeded only very gradually in withdrawing the mass of the working people from the influence of the democrats whose tail they formed in the beginning of the revolution. But in due time the indecision weakness and cowardice of the democratic leaders did the rest, and it may now be said to be one of the principal results of the last years' convulsions, that wherever the working class is concentrated in anything like considerable masses, they are entirely freed from that democratic influence which led them into an endless series of blunders and misfortunes during 1848 and 1849." (F. Engels, MESW, vol. 1, p. 332.)

Rottenness of Liberals

The rottenness of the bourgeois liberals, and their counterrevolutionary role in the bourgeois-democratic revolution, was explained quite clearly by Marx and Engels. In his article *The Bourgeoisie and the Counter-revolution* (1848), Marx writes:

"The German bourgeoisie has developed so slothfully, cravenly and slowly that at the moment when it menacingly faced feudalism and absolutism it saw itself menacingly faced by the proletariat and all factions of the burgers whose interests and ideas were akin to those of the proletariat. And it saw inimically arrayed not only a class *behind* it but all Europe *before* it. The Prussian bourgeoisie was not, as the French of 1789 had been, the class which represented the *whole* of modern society *vis-à-vis* the representatives of the old society, the monarchy and the nobility. It had sunk to the level of a kind of social estate, as distinctly opposed to the crown as to the people, eager to be in the opposition to both, irresolute against each of its opponents, taken severally, because it always saw both of them before or behind it; inclined to betray the people and compromise with the crowned representative of the old society because it itself already belonged to the old society." (K. Marx, MESW, vol. 1, pp. 140-1.)

The bourgeoisie, Marx explains, did not come to power as a result of its own revolutionary exertions, but as a result of the movement of the masses in which it played no role: "The Prussian bourgeoisie was hurled to the height of state power, however not in the manner it had desired, by a peaceful bargain with the crown but by a revolution". (K. Marx, ibid, p. 138.)

As a matter of fact Wolfe Tone, the great Irish revolutionary, had come to a similar conclusion 200 years ago when he wrote, "Our freedom must be had at all hazards. If the men of property will not help us they must fall; we will free ourselves by the aid of that large and respectable class of the community – the men of no property."

The situation is clearer still today. The national bourgeoisie in the colonial countries, and Ireland was England's first colony, entered into the scene of history too late, when the world had already been divided up between a few imperialist powers. It was not able to play any progressive role and was born completely subordinated to its former colonial masters. The weak and degenerate bourgeoisie in Asia, Latin America and Africa is too dependent on foreign capital and imperialism, to carry society forward. It is tied with a thousand threads, not only to foreign capital, but also with the class of landowners, with which it forms a reactionary bloc that represents a bulwark against progress. Whatever differences may exist between these elements are insignificant in comparison with the fear that unites them against the masses. Only the proletariat, allied with the poor peasants and urban poor, can solve the problems of society in these countries by taking power into its own hands, expropriating the imperialists and the bourgeoisie, and beginning the task of transforming society on socialist lines.

By setting itself at the head of the nation, leading the oppressed layers of society (the urban and rural petty-bourgeoisie), the proletariat could take power and then carry through the tasks of the bourgeois-democratic revolution (mainly land reform unification and the liberation of the country from foreign domination). However, once having come to power, the proletariat would not stop there but would start to implement socialist measures of expropriation of the capitalists. And as these tasks cannot be solved in one country alone, especially not in a backward country, this would be the beginning of the world revolution. Thus the revolution is "permanent" in two senses: because it starts with the bourgeois tasks and continues with the socialist ones, and because it starts in one country and continues at an international level.

How does this apply to contemporary Ireland? Here there can be no illusions of "stages" which must be achieved before the workers can struggle to take power and begin the socialist transformation of society. The idea of solving the border question first, and postponing the struggle for socialism until later has proven over many years to be a trap masquerading as a realistic policy. The border question, and the other social, economic and political questions facing Irish society, cannot be solved within the framework of the capitalist system. The Irish bourgeoisie can play no progressive part in trying to solve these problems. Throughout their history they have infamously betrayed the cause of Ireland. They are intimately bound up with British and US imperialism. Their system, which cannot provide for the basic needs of the majority - in terms of health, education, housing and the other minimums of civilisation - is a breeding ground for sectarianism. Indeed the weed of sectarianism, planted by British imperialism has been watered and fed by the inability of the capitalist system to provide for the majority. Neither the capitalist class nor the capitalist system can resolve any of the problems facing Ireland. Only one class remains capable of playing a revolutionary role and that is the working class. A revolutionary movement on the part of the Irish working class would not be confined by any borders. The united struggle of the Irish workers would be an inspiration to the working class in Britain and across Europe.

Permanent Revolution

One hundred years ago the theory of the permanent revolution was the most complete answer to the reformist and class collaborationist position of the right wing of the Russian workers' movement, the Mensheviks. Far from being out of date however these ideas are perhaps even more relevant to the current world situation than they were when they were first written. Therefore it is necessary to restate these ideas, at least in outline.

The two-stage theory was developed by the Mensheviks as their perspective for the Russian revolution. In essence it states that, since the tasks of the revolution are those of the national democratic *bourgeois* revolution, the leadership of the revolution must be taken by the national democratic *bourgeoisie*. For his part, Lenin agreed with Trotsky that the Russian Liberals could not carry out the bourgeois-democratic revolution, and that this task could only be carried out by the proletariat in alliance with the poor peasantry. Following in the footsteps of Marx, who had described the bourgeois "democratic party" as "far more dangerous to the workers than the previous liberals", Lenin explained that the Russian bourgeoisie, far from being an ally of the workers, would *inevitably* side with the counter-revolution.

"The bourgeoisie in the mass", he wrote in 1905, "will inevitably turn towards the counter-revolution, and against the people as soon as its narrow, selfish interests are met, as soon as it 'recoils' from consistent democracy (and it is already recoiling from it!)." (Lenin, *Collected Works*, vol. 9, p. 98.)

What class, in Lenin's view, could lead the bourgeois-democratic revolution? "There remains 'the people', that is, the proletariat and the peasantry. The proletariat alone can be relied on to march on to the end, for it goes far beyond the democratic revolution. That is why the proletariat fights in the forefront for a republic and contemptuously rejects stupid and unworthy advice to take into account the possibility of the bourgeoisie recoiling" (Lenin, ibid.)

In all of Lenin's speeches and writings, the counter-revolutionary role of the bourgeois-democratic Liberals is stressed time and time again. However, up until 1917, he did not believe that the Russian workers would come to power before the socialist revolution in the West—a perspective that only Trotsky defended before 1917, when it was fully adopted by Lenin in his April theses. The correctness of the permanent revolution was triumphantly demonstrated by the October Revolution itself.

Connolly famously described the class forces in the Irish revolution and the struggle for national liberation as follows: "Only the Irish working class remain as the incorruptible inheritors of the fight for freedom in Ireland."

In the permanent revolution Trotsky applies this idea generally, that in the modern epoch only the working class could solve the tasks of the bourgeois-democratic revolution, including the national question, and that it would do this by taking power into its own hands. This prognosis was shown to be correct in 1917 when the Russian proletariat took power in a backward, predominantly peasant country. The Russian working class joined forces with the workers of the formerly oppressed nationalities and began the task of the socialist transformation of society. True, they did not ultimately succeed, because of the isolation of the revolution in conditions of frightful backwardness. But that is another question.

The point is that, once they had taken power, the Russian proletariat solved the national question easily, as a by-product of the socialist revolution.

What was true for Russia was a hundred times truer for Ireland even a century ago. As Connolly explained the bourgeoisie and the petit bourgeoisie could not solve the national question in Ireland, because they were tied by a thousand threads to the bourgeoisie of Britain. The working class was the only force capable of solving these national democratic tasks, but only *en route* to the socialist transformation of society, as part of the socialist revolution.

Part Two

Historical role of bourgeois nationalism

Everywhere we look in the world we can see how the so-called national bourgeoisie has failed to solve the national question. Ireland is no exception. The history of Ireland since the 18th century shows that the bourgeoisie is not capable of waging a serious struggle against imperialism or of solving the national question. The weak and toothless Irish bourgeoisie arrived too late on the stage of history. It was unable to compete with the giant across the water, which in any case was determined to prevent the rise of a powerful rival in Ireland, which it wanted to keep as a backward agrarian colony.

From the very beginning the Irish bourgeoisie was incapable of playing an independent role or of developing Ireland as a strong and independent nation. It was always content to play second fiddle to the English landlords, bankers and capitalists, while grumbling about its disadvantaged situation. At every decisive moment it betrayed the cause of Ireland in favour of its selfish economic interests. On those rare occasions when it grudgingly supported the struggle against English domination, it did so only in order to keep the masses under control, to apply the brakes and in the end to sell out to England.

It is therefore impossible to understand the national liberation struggle without analysing its class content. In their writings we discover that Connolly, Lenin and Trotsky adopted the same attitude towards the national bourgeoisie. Connolly wrote: "The working men fought, the capitalists sold out, the lawyers bluffed." (James Connolly, *Labour in Irish History*, p. 52.) These words sum up two hundred years of Irish history down to the present day. As early as the 18th century, it is worth repeating, the great Irish revolutionary democrat Wolfe Tone stated that Ireland could only be freed by the "men of no property".

These were prophetic words! The conduct of the bourgeois nationalist leaders throughout history is not at all accidental. Starting with Henry Grattan, the well-to-do proponents of Irish nationalism have always defended their own selfish class interests and always preferred a deal with the imperialist masters rather than allow power to pass to the Irish workers and poor farmers. Right down to the present day, when the 26 Counties have had a caricature of "independence" for over 80 years, it feels far more comfortable with the rich and powerful in England than with its own working class, let alone the movement in the Six Counties, which it sees as a liability.

The real history of the national liberation struggle in Ireland begins with the French revolution. The destiny of Ireland has repeatedly been shaped by revolutionary developments on a world scale. Even before the French revolution, the first impulse to the Irish national liberation movement came from the American Revolution. The loss of the American colonies showed that England was not invincible. It also disposed London to make concessions to the emerging Irish bourgeoisie, as it did in the Navigation Acts of 1778. Emboldened, the mainly Protestant Irish bourgeoisie pressed for more rights. In 1779, when the Dublin Parliament met, all the MPs pledged to wear only Irish manufactured clothes. This showed the real interests of these gentlemen, who organised the Irish Volunteers - an armed force of 80,000 at its peak, pledged to secure Ireland's rights from England.

However, from the beginning the Irish bourgeoisie was concerned first and foremost with their narrow class point of view. The "rights" they aspired to mainly concerned their trading interests. The Irish parliament passed a motion declaring "only by a free trade could this nation be saved from impending ruin." The feeble administration of Lord North in London, chastened by defeat in America, backed down and conceded free trade for Ireland. The flood tide of "Protestant Ireland" came in 1782, when the Volunteers at Dungannon proclaimed what is now known as "Grattan's Parliament". Again London appeared to give in, whereupon the Irish bourgeoisie showed its gratitude by *voting one hundred pounds to the British navy*, and another *fifty thousand to Henry Grattan* who was supposed to have clinched the deal. This little detail sets the tone for the whole business: it shows the venal and cowardly character of the Irish bourgeoisie, which behaved like a faithful dog licking the hand of the master who was kind enough to throw it a bone. It also shows that the services of those who pretended to stand for "Irish Freedom" always came with a price tag attached.

Grattan made a famous speech, ending: "Ireland is now a nation. In that character I hail her and, bowing in her august presence, I say *esto perpetua*." In reality, this was all a hollow show. Grattan's parliament lasted only 18 years. The "new constitution" rested on an unreformed parliament of wealthy Protestants. How could this be, when the great majority of Irish people were Catholics and oppressed peasants? The Parliament was corrupt and rotten. This is what Connolly wrote about Grattan:

"Mr. Grattan would have given the vote to any man who owned property, irrespective of religion, and he opposed its extension to any propertyless man. In the Irish House of Commons he bitterly denounced the United Irishmen [....], for proposing universal suffrage, which he declared would ruin the country and destroy all order.

"It will be seen that Mr. Grattan was the ideal capitalist statesman; his spirit was the spirit of the bourgeoisie incarnate. He cared more for the interests of property than for human rights or for the supremacy of any religion." (Connolly, ibid, p. 55.)

These lines accurately express the nature of *all* bourgeois nationalists everywhere - not just in Ireland. Their inevitable tendency to betray the people and compromise with imperialism is not an accident. It flows from their class interests and their position as exploiters of the working class and the peasantry. *It is impossible to begin to understand the history of the Irish national struggle unless from a class point of view.* That was always the standpoint of the Marxist James Connolly.

"The Parliament of 1782" was regarded by the real Irish revolutionaries as a sell-out, much as we regard the so-called peace process today. It was a deal reached by the bourgeois leadership with London behind the backs of the people and against their interests. By contrast, the most advanced elements of Irish society, inspired by the French Revolution, stood for a revolutionary solution, based on the self-movement of the masses - the "men of no property".

Wolfe Tone

In September 1791, Theobald Wolfe Tone - who came from a Protestant background - published a pamphlet entitled *An Argument on behalf of the Catholics of Ireland*. This pamphlet, with its revolutionary spirit and its biting characterisation of the "glorious revolution of 1782" *was deliberately suppressed by the Irish bourgeois nationalists* and was only republished in 1897. This is typical of the way the bourgeois and petty bourgeois nationalists seek to distort and suppress the real history of Ireland's national liberation struggle and conceal its class nature. *Wolfe Tone is presented as a revolutionary "icon", but the true nature of his ideas is suppressed and hidden from the new generation of Irish youth - exactly as happened with Connolly.*

Writing about Wolfe Tone, and unwittingly about himself, Connolly remarked, "Apostles of freedom are ever idolised when dead, but crucified when living." The first duty of Irish Marxists must be to rescue the memory of the great revolutionary leaders and martyrs of the past and explain to the new generation the traditions of the Irish people. This is the only way in which we can finally break the pernicious stranglehold of bourgeois and middle class nationalism on the movement - the prior condition for future victory.

From the very beginning, the policies of the bourgeois nationalists were challenged by courageous men and women who understood the need to unite the national liberation struggle with the struggle for social liberation. In his pamphlet Wolfe Tone wrote: "the revolution of 1782 was the most bungling, imperfect business that ever threw ridicule on a lofty epithet, by assuming it unworthily. It is not pleasant for any Irishman to make such a concession, but it cannot be helped if such a truth will have it so. It is much better that we should know and feel our real state, than delude ourselves or be gulled by our enemies with praises which we do not deserve, or imaginary blessings which we do not enjoy." (Connolly, ibid, p. 57.)

How relevant these lines sound today! The tendency to prettify reality and to conceal things under false names ("revolution", "national liberation", "armed struggle", etc.) has been a constant feature of the history of Ireland ever since the days of Wolfe Tone. It is necessary to cut across this thick fog and – like James Connolly - *call things by their correct names.*

"The Revolution of 1782", writes Connolly, "was a Revolution which enabled Irishmen to sell at a much higher price their honour, their integrity, and the interests of their country; it was a Revolution which, while at a stroke it doubled the value of every borough-monger in the kingdom, left three-fourths of our countrymen slaves as it found them, and the government of Ireland in the base and wicked and contemptible hands who had spent their lives in degrading and plundering her; nay, some of whom had given their last vote decidedly, though hopelessly, against this, our famous Revolution." (Connolly, ibid, p. 58.)

The United Irishmen linked the national liberation struggle with the tasks of the social emancipation of the masses. Connolly cited the movement as "a revolutionary party openly declaring their revolutionary sympathies but limiting their first demand to a popular measure such as *would enfranchise the masses, upon whose support their ultimate success must rest."* (Connolly, ibid).

Inspired by the revolutionary democratic ideals of the French Revolution, Tone and the United Irishmen demanded equal representation of all the people in parliament, irrespective of class or creed. They waged a *class war* against the aristocracy. The movement to unite the masses terrified the aristocracy and proprietors - English and Irish, Catholic and Protestant - against the United Irishmen. The latter were not narrow nationalists, but revolutionary democrats and internationalists who actively sought - and obtained - contacts with revolutionaries, not only in France, but also in England and Scotland. Belfast was then a hotbed of revolution and the seat of the first society of United Irishmen. They worked out a revolutionary programme of democratic demands, including the enfranchisement of all the people, making no distinction between taxpayers and non-taxpayers. As Connolly comments:

"Nothing less would have succeeded in causing Protestant and Catholic masses to shake hands over the bloody chasm of religious hatreds, nothing less will accomplish the same result in our day among the Irish workers." (Connolly, ibid, p. 80.)

The United Irishmen, as Connolly explained were both *revolutionary democrats and internationalists*. They stood for a popular revolution that would unite all the oppressed masses of Ireland, irrespective of religious differences:

"The Protestant workman and tenant was learning that the Pope of Rome was a very unreal and shadowy danger compared to the social power of his employer or landlord, and the Catholic tenant was awakening to a perception of the fact that under the new social order the Catholic landlord represented the Mass less than the rent-roll." (Connolly, ibid, p. 70.)

In the end, however, the movement of the Volunteers was "a chapter of great opportunities lost, of popular confidence betrayed", as Connolly said. And the same thing could be said of every subsequent phase of the Irish national liberation struggle right up to today. Despite all their heroism, the United Irishmen were defeated. Why? *Because in the moment of truth, class loyalties always prove more powerful than religious or national affiliation.* The wealthy Irish property owners felt, correctly, that they had much more in common with the English propertied classes than the revolutionary Irish poor.

The Betrayal

The uprising, which was led by *Protestant* revolutionary democrats, representing the "men of no property", was betrayed by a *Catholic* silk-merchant, Thomas Reynolds, who provided the government with advance warning and a copy of a paper of the Supreme Executive of the United Irishmen, showing that no less than 279,000 men were sworn and armed to rise. The rising was aborted and its supporters put down with great barbarity. Peasants were tortured to reveal the hiding places of arms. Tone cut his own wrists to avoid being hanged.

One contemporary reports:

"Numbers have been flogged who have been caught with pikes, and all but one peached and discovered. I have seen none of these floggings, but it is terrible to hear the perseverance of these madmen. Some have received three hundred lashes before they would discover where the pikes were concealed." (P. Johnson, *Ireland, a Concise History*, p. 81.)

Following the suppression of the Volunteers (the "military wing" of the United Irishmen) in March 1793, the movement went underground and embarked on a period of reconstruction. This was based on social radicalism and, following Wolfe Tone's advice, they began to enlist "the men of no property", the journeymen and wage-earners who were already well organised in combinations, especially in the Dublin area. A network of workingmen's "reading clubs" was formed, under the influence of the French Revolution and Thomas Paine's *The Rights of Man*.

Divide and rule

The British imperialists had received a rude shock in 1798, and decided that they would have to take serious steps to ensure that it was not repeated. The Act of Union of 1801 brought Ireland under the direct rule of Westminster. But the revolutionary events of 1798 made the British ruling class aware of the mortal threat posed by a united movement of the Irish Protestants and Catholics. Henceforth all their efforts were concentrated on destroying that unity.

A reign of terror was organised against the mainly Catholic peasantry. But the main weapon upon which England relied to destroy the Irish revolution was the fomenting of divisions between Catholics and Protestants. In the words of General Knox, the commander of the British garrison in Ireland: "I have arranged to increase the animosity between Orangemen and the United Irish. Upon that animosity depends the safety of the centre counties of the North." (Quoted in Liam de Paor, *Divided Ulster*, p. 57, our emphasis.)

The Orange Order was born in Armagh in 1795 as part of a campaign to terrorise the Catholics and deny them full citizenship rights. However, the Order was directed not just at Catholics but also "disloyal" Protestants. It was actively backed by the British state in the years leading up to the 1798 rebellion precisely in order to drive a wedge between ordinary Catholics and Protestants.

The 12th of July was chosen as the key date for Protestant celebrations, ostensibly to mark the Battle of the Boyne, but the real reason was to provide an alternative attraction to the celebration of Bastille day. From the very beginning the 12th of July celebrations were marked by sectarian attacks against Catholics. In 1795 up to 7,000 Catholics were driven out of Armagh by Orange Order pogroms. However, it is not generally known that many expelled Catholic families were sheltered by Presbyterian United Irishmen in Belfast and later Antrim and Down, and the (mostly) Protestant leadership of the United Irishmen sent lawyers to prosecute on behalf of the victims of Orange attacks. They also sent special missions to the area to undermine the Orange Order's influence.

At this time there was a bitter struggle between landlords and tenants in the area. Commenting on this the Anglican Archbishop of Armagh said "the worst of this is that it stands to unite Protestant and Papist, and whenever that happens, good-bye to the English interest in Ireland."

The Orange Order played a key part in undermining the 1798 rebellion. At the time General John Knox described the Orange Order as "the only barrier we have against the United Irishmen." After the failed rebellion he wrote, "the institution of the Orange Order was of infinite use".

Paradoxically the Orange Order was originally opposed to the Union, whereas the Catholic Church supported it. The Catholic bishops and priests, not for the last time, backed the British authorities against the United Irishmen whose revolutionary and atheistic ideas were anathema to them. In January 1799, an assembly of Catholic bishops accepted a government offer of state provision for the Catholic clergy, in return for letting the state confirm Episcopal elections and the appointment of parish priests. In the end, of course, they received next to nothing.

Today we stand firmly on the basis of the revolutionary traditions of Wolfe Tone and the United Irishmen. We understand that Ireland will never be united and free unless and until the working class places itself at the head of the liberation struggle and links this firmly with the task of the social revolution. We also understand that the prior condition for the socialist transformation of society is the maximum unity of the working class, cutting across all lines of nationality, religion and gender.

It is absolutely false, defeatist and reactionary to argue that it is impossible to achieve the unity of the Catholic and Protestant working people. That was done in the past by the United Irishmen and by Connolly and Larkin. There is no reason why it should not be done again. What is necessary is to fight on the basis of those social and class demands that are capable of uniting the working class against landlordism and capitalism. *What is needed is a class policy.* To quote Connolly:

"To accomplish this union, and make it a living force in the life of the nation, there was required the activity of a revolutionist with statesmanship enough to find a common point upon which the two elements could unite, and some great event, dramatic enough in its character, to arrest the attention of all and fire them with a common feeling." (Connolly, op cit, pp. 70-1.)

The cardinal lesson of all Irish history ever since 1798 is quite clear: the division between Catholic and Protestant was the main weapon used by imperialism and reaction to weaken and undermine the struggle of the people for their national and social emancipation. The conclusion is likewise inescapable: *every step that tends to increase the unity of the working class of the two communities is progressive and must be supported, every action that tends to increase the division serves the interests of imperialism and reaction and must be rejected.*

After the defeat of the United Irishmen in 1798 came the so-called Emmet conspiracy, which was even more distinctly democratic, international and popular in content. It had a more working class composition. Significantly, once more, the movement was betrayed to the authorities by middle class Catholic "nationalists". The Rev. Thomas Barry, parish priest of Mallow, discovered the plot in confession and ordered his parishioner to reveal it to the military.

"Emmet is the most idolised, the most universally praised of all Irish martyrs; it is, therefore, worthy of note that in the proclamation he drew up to be issued in the name of the 'Provisional Government of Ireland' the first article decrees the wholesale confiscation of church property and the nationalisation of the same, and the second and third decrees forbid and declare void the transfer of all landed property, bonds, debentures and public securities, until the national government is established and the national will upon them is declared."

Connolly comments on this:

"Two things are thus established - viz. that Emmet believed that the 'national will' was superior to property rights, and could abolish them at will; and also that he realised that *the producing classes could not be expected to rally to the revolution unless given to understand that it meant their freedom from social as well as from political bondage*." (Connolly, ibid, pp. 86-7, our emphasis)

These lines are of crucial importance. Their meaning is quite clear and unambiguous: *that the struggle for political freedom - including national liberation - is unthinkable unless it is linked to the social emancipation of the working class*. This is the great lesson which Connolly derived from a painstaking reading of Irish history. His opinion of Emmet is thus different to that of the professional eulogisers who habitually gather like vultures around the coffin of a dead revolutionary - that "crop of orators who know all about Emmet's martyrdom, and nothing about his principles." (Connolly, ibid.)

These lines could be said equally of the historical destiny of Connolly himself.

Catholic Emancipation

The national oppression of the Irish people was made more bitter by the introduction of a religious element after the Reformation. In the nineteenth century, the enforced collection of a religious tax (the tithe) by the Protestant Episcopalian Church was a particularly brutal measure, detested by the Catholic peasantry. Protestant clergy would collect this hated tax accompanied by police and soldiers. The peasants resisted, leading to clashes with the army, where peasants were wounded or killed. The masses organised secret societies like the *Ribbon* and *Whiteboy* societies to resist these impositions, but the middle class politicians who spoke in the name of the Irish people gave no support to this movement.

In 1818 the Protestant Church founded a society to develop the Irish language as a means of obtaining conversions. Its members challenged the Catholic priests to debates in Gaelic on doctrinal differences. *As a result of this Protestant interest in Gaelic, the Catholic Church threw all its weight behind the teaching of English in all elementary schools.* This sealed the fate of the Irish language as a spoken language. Thus, the spread of education undermined the language, which was further decimated by the effects of mass emigration after the Famine.

Daniel O'Connell was typical of the middle class political exploiters of the Irish people - "those well-fed snobs", as Connolly described them - who leaned on the masses to further their own careers, only to abandon them as soon as their narrow interests were served. His first act was to repudiate Wolfe Tone and his companions as "criminals":

" 'As to '98', he said, 'we leave the weak and wicked men who considered force and sanguinary violence as part of their resources for ameliorating our institutions, and the equally wicked and designing wretches who fomented the Rebellion and made it explode... We leave both of these classes of miscreants to the contempt and indignation of mankind.' " (P. Johnson, op cit, p. 92.)

O'Connell benefited from the wave of agitation that swept across England in the early 1830s. This in turn was a partial reflection of the July Revolution in France which had overthrown the Bourbons in 1830. As always, democratic reform in Britain was a by-product of revolution in Europe. But whatever concessions are made by the ruling class are always partial and niggardly. The 1832 Reform Act for Ireland did not democratise the vote at all, restricting it to ten pounds householders in towns and twenty pounds leaseholders in counties. What it did do was to enfranchise the Catholic middle class in the towns, preparing the way for the 1840 Municipal Reform Act which abolished the corrupt old Protestant corporations and allowed the Catholics to take over the towns and cities. O'Connell himself became mayor of Dublin.

This wily and unprincipled opportunist leaned on the Irish masses to further his own career, speaking to mass meetings of up to 250,000 people, demanding an Irish parliament, but all the while upholding the class interests of the capitalists against the workers and the poor. In the English parliament, this consummate representative of Capital opposed the introduction of the Factory Acts aimed at lightening the burden of labour, on the grounds that "they (Parliament) had legislated against the nature of things and against the rights of industry." "Let them not", he said, "be guilty of the childish folly of regulating the labour of adults, and go about parading before the world *their ridiculous humanity,* which would end up by converting their manufacturers into beggars." (Connolly, op cit, p. 125.)

While making demagogic speeches appealing to Irish nationalism, O'Connell was ingratiating himself to the English Establishment. His whole mentality can be seen in his speech at Mullingar on 14th May 1843:

"They say we want separation from England, but what I want is to prevent separation taking place. There is not a man in existence more loyally attached than I am to the Queen - God bless her. The present state of Ireland is nearly unendurable, and if the people of Ireland had not some person like me to lead them in the paths of peace and constitutional exertion, I am afraid of the result (*hear!*) While I live I will stand by the throne (hear, hear!)." (P. Johnson, op cit, p. 94.)

Authentic voice

This is the authentic voice of the Irish bourgeoisie - *unprincipled, reactionary, cowardly, grovelling*. The move to obtain rights for Catholics was aimed at improving the position and furthering the careers of people like O'Connell, not the masses, as Connolly points out:

"The Catholic middle, professional and landed class by Catholic Emancipation had the way open to them for all the snug berths in the disposal of the Government; the Catholics of the poorer class as a result of the same Act were doomed to extermination..." (Connolly, op cit, p. 102.)

After the Emancipation, the Irish masses were no better off than before, as we see from the declaration of a witness from the labourers to the *Ribbon Association*:

"What good did the Emancipation do for us? Are we better clothed or fed, or are our children better clothed or fed? Are we not as naked as we were, and eating dry potatoes when we can get them? Let us notice the farmers to give us better food and better wages, and not give so much to the landlord, and more to the workman; we must not be letting them be turning the poor people off the ground." (Connolly, ibid, p. 104)

Here is the real voice of the Irish people, not the sleek lawyers' arguments of the middle class nationalists, under whose cloak of "patriotism" was always concealed the most barefaced and cynical self-interest. Connolly observes dryly:

"It is difficult to see how a promised Repeal of the Union some time in the future could have been any use to the starving men of Clare, especially when they knew that their fathers had been starved, evicted and tyrannised over before just as they were *after* the Union." (Connolly, ibid, p. 103.)

This shows the abyss that has always separated socialists from nationalism. Our standpoint has always been a class standpoint and no other. Our aim is the political and social emancipation of the working class, as the only way to guarantee a decent life for all. Insofar as we fight for national liberation it is as part of a far broader struggle against capitalism and imperialism on a world scale. Under no circumstances will we accept the subordination of the fight for the interests of the working class to the alleged interests of the Nation - an artificial formula which seeks to hide from view the never-ending struggle between Capital and Labour.

Again this was always the position of Connolly:

"It may be argued that the ideal of the Socialist Republic, implying as it does, a complete economic and political revolution, would be sure to alienate all our middle-class and aristocratic supporters who would dread the loss of their property and their privileges. What does this objection mean? That we must conciliate the privileged classes in Ireland! But you can only disarm their hostility by assuring them that in a *free* Ireland their privileges will not be 'interfered with'. That is to say, you must guarantee that when Ireland is free of foreign domination, the green-coated Irish soldiers will guard the fraudulent gains of the capitalist and the landlord from the 'thin hands of the poor' just as remorselessly and just as effectually as the scarlet coated emissaries of England do today.

"On no other basis will the classes unite with you. Do you expect the masses to fight for this ideal?" (*Shan Van Vocht*, January, 1897.)

Part Three

Feargus O'Connor and the Fenians

All history has shown that the bourgeoisie is only concerned with its selfish class interests, and merely uses the national flag to conceal this fact and blind and disorient the masses, until the moment when it finally stabs them in the back. When Feargus O'Connor, a sincere Irish democrat, attempted to win over O'Connell, he soon realised the real state of affairs:

"He earnestly strove to impress this view upon O'Connell, only to find that in the latter class feeling was much stronger than desire for Irish National freedom and that he, O'Connell, felt himself to be *much more akin to the propertied class of England than to the working class of Ireland.*" (Connolly, ibid, p. 125, my emphasis.)

That is the crux of the matter. *What is decisive is class interest.* In the final analysis, the bourgeoisie of any nation will always unite with the bourgeoisie of an "enemy" state against its own working class. For all the theatrics and "patriotic" demagogy, the likes of O'Connell (and there have been many O'Connells in Irish history, and there are at present) will always feel more at home with the bankers, lawyers and businessmen of London than with the working people of their own land. Thus, when we accuse them of "betraying the cause", we must add that, in reality, they have always been, and remain to this day, remarkably faithful to their cause: *the cause of Rent, Interest and Profit.*

The national struggle of the Irish people in the 19th century unfolded against a background of falling living standards and increasing class struggle. Marx pointed out that between 1849 and 1869, while wages in Ireland had increased by 50 or 60 per cent, the prices of all necessities had more than doubled. Poverty and hunger were widespread. But a similar situation existed in Great Britain. The basis was thus laid for a revolutionary alliance of the English and Irish working class, as both Marx and Connolly pointed out. But the Fenians were regarded with hatred by the wealthy Irish nationalists and the Catholic Church, which condemned them. The Archbishop of Dublin, Dr. Paul Cullen, even refused to allow them a Christian burial. Connolly comments:

"It is notorious that Fenianism was regarded with unconcealed aversion, not to say deadly hatred, not merely by the landlords and the ruling class, but by the Catholic clergy, the middle class Catholics, and the great majority of the farming classes. *It was in fact only among the youngest and most intelligent of the labouring classes, of the young men of the largest towns and cities engaged in the humbler walks of mercantile life, of the artisan and working classes, that it found favour.*" (Connolly, ibid, p. 161.)

The Fenians were the most advanced wing of the Irish revolutionary democratic movement. They were heroic and showed socialist inclinations, but they also made mistakes. Marx and Engels naturally supported them but at the same time they severely criticised them for their adventurist tactics, their terrorist tendencies, their national narrowness and their refusal to accept the need to link up with the English workers' movement. On November 29th, 1867, Engels wrote to Marx:

"As regards the Fenians you are quite right. The beastliness of the English must not make us forget that the leaders of this sect are mostly asses and partly exploiters and we cannot in any way make ourselves responsible for the stupidities which occur in every conspiracy. And they are certain to happen."

Engels was soon proved right. Just two weeks later, on the 13th December 1867, a group of Fenians set off an explosion in London's Clerkenwell Prison in an unsuccessful attempt to free their imprisoned comrades. The explosion destroyed several neighbouring houses and wounded 120 people. Predictably, the incident unleashed a wave of anti-Irish feeling in the population. The following day Marx wrote indignantly to Engels:

"The last exploit of the Fenians in Clerkenwell was a very stupid thing. The London masses, who have shown great sympathy for Ireland, will be made wild by it and driven into the arms of the government party. One cannot expect the London proletariat to allow themselves to be blown up in honour of the Fenian emissaries. There is always a kind of fatality about such a secret, melodramatic sort of conspiracy."

A few days later, on December 19th, Engels replied as follows: "The stupid affair in Clerkenwell was obviously the work of a few specialised fanatics; it is the misfortune of all conspiracies that they lead to such stupidities, because 'after all, something must happen, after all something must be done'. In particular, there has been a lot of bluster in America about this blowing up and arson business, and then a few asses come and instigate such nonsense. Moreover, these cannibals are generally the greatest cowards, like this Allen, who seems to have already turned Queen's evidence, and then the idea of liberating Ireland by setting a London tailor's shop on fire!" (*Marx and Engels on Ireland*, p.149, Progress Publishers 1971)

We should cherish and respect the memory of the Fenians, but we must not repeat their mistakes. The tactics of individual terrorism alienated the English working class and proved completely counterproductive. Instead of furthering the Irish cause it harmed it. Unfortunately, the right wing of the Republican movement repeated all these mistakes in the last period, and produced even more fatal results. The idea that "after all, something must be done" does not constitute a strategy or a policy, and, despite its appeal to impatient elements, always has the most negative consequences for the movement as a whole. The way to hell is paved with good intentions.

Michael Davitt and the Land League

Throughout all this period the landowning class in Ireland formed a bulwark of reaction in Britain itself. A bitter class war raged in the Irish countryside, and the national question was inseparably linked to the land question. In the latter half of the 19th century, the land question was the burning question in Ireland. Gladstone made concessions in the hope of getting the support of the Irish group in the Westminster parliament. The Land Act of 1870 was a mild reform intended to improve the lot of the downtrodden Irish peasantry. But the collapse of the income of the Irish peasants as a result of the economic depression meant that the mass of peasants gained nothing from it. What use were tenants' rights if rents could not be paid? The real issue was not addressed: the ownership of land.

The landed interests in Ireland combined with the English Tories to sabotage the Liberal plan and crush the peasants' revolt. In order to split and destroy the movement for land reform, they deliberately encouraged religious sectarianism. The Lord Lieutenant, the Earl of Mayo, wrote to Disraeli:

"Ireland is an infernal country to manage... Impartiality is impossible, statesmanship wholly out of place. The only way to govern is the old plan (which I will not attempt) of taking up violently one faction against the other, putting them like fighting-cocks, and then backing one. I wish you would send me to India. Ireland is the grave of every reputation." (P. Johnson, op cit, p. 135.)

Michael Davitt came from a family of poor dispossessed peasants. He set up the Land League in 1879. The Land League advised the peasants to pay only what they considered a fair rent, and if that was refused, to pay nothing. Evictions were to be resisted (Davitt's own family had been evicted) and anyone who took over an evicted farm was to be boycotted. This was a militant campaign against landed interests in Ireland - the backbone of reaction.

The agrarian movement was met with vicious state repression, embodied in the Coercion Laws. This merely stiffened the resolve of the masses, who fought back bravely, risking eviction and imprisonment. As usual, all the risks and dangers were run by the poor peasants. But the fruits were reaped by the English Liberals and Irish bourgeois Home Rulers who climbed to power on the backs of the revolutionary Irish peasantry. Connolly wrote:

"... When the rising tide of victorious revolt in Ireland compelled the Liberal Party to give a half-hearted acquiescence to the demands of the Irish peasantry, and the Home Rule-Liberal alliance was consummated, the Irish businessmen in Great Britain came to the front, and succeeded in worming themselves into all positions of trust and leadership in the Irish organisations. One of the first and most bitter fruits of that alliance was the use of the Irish vote against the candidates of the Socialist and Labour Parties." (Connolly, op cit, p. 166).

In the 1880 election, 65 Irish nationalists were returned to Westminster, thirty of them supporters of Parnell. Gladstone, who became prime minister, carried out a land reform, but coupled it with a Coercion Bill directed against the militant actions of the village poor. The middle class peasants were given a pat on the back, and the poor received a kick in the teeth. The 1881 Land Act was so complicated that it was said that only Gladstone himself and his parliamentary draftsman could understand it. But the 100,000 poor peasants who were in arrears and threatened with eviction, who were excluded from the Act, could understand it only too well.

"As we have again and again pointed out, the Irish question is a social question, the whole age-long fight of the Irish people against their oppressors resolves itself, in the last analysis, into a fight for the mastery of the means of life, the sources of production, in Ireland." (Connolly, ibid, p. 167.)

Michael Davitt adopted a consistent revolutionary class policy in his agitation on the land question. He appealed to the peasants on a class basis, thus cutting the ground from under the feet of those who sought to divide the masses with the poison of religious sectarianism. In 1881 the Land league was able to hold a meeting in the local Orange hall at Loughgall. Davitt told the crowd that the "landlords of Ireland are all of one religion - their God is mammon and rack-rents, and evictions their only morality, while the toilers of the fields, whether Orangemen, Catholics, Presbyterians or Methodists are the victims."

Like all the consistent fighters for Irish freedom, Davitt strove to unite the downtrodden and oppressed on class lines, cutting across religious and sectarian divisions, while the enemies of freedom strove to exacerbate the divisions. The danger posed to the Establishment by class unity set the alarm bells ringing and the Grand Orange Lodge of Ireland responded with a manifesto claiming that the Land League was a conspiracy against property rights, Protestantism, civil and religious liberty and the British constitution. When the question was put this way the Orange Order fulfilled its role and went on to provide the scab labour, which attempted to harvest Captain Boycott's crops.

This revolutionary movement of the Irish peasantry threatened the landlord class - the basis of English rule in Ireland. The latter took determined action to undermine and destroy the movement of the masses. *For this purpose they recruited the support of the Irish nationalist middle class and the Catholic Church whose fear of the revolutionary movement of the masses has always been far greater than their attachment to Ireland.* The increase in repression led to a drop of "agrarian crimes" from 4,438 in 1881 to 870 in 1883.

In the end the Land League was *sold out* by its middle-class leaders. Connolly, who took a great interest in this question, advocated a revolutionary solution to the land problem, based on a revolutionary alliance between the working class and the peasantry to defeat both imperialism and capitalism. However, the prior condition for a revolutionary solution of the agrarian problem in Ireland was that the poor Irish peasant should break with the middle class politicians and join forces with the only genuinely revolutionary class - the proletariat.

The Land League, which sought the diminution of landlordism and the promotion of peasant-proprietorship, was ultimately banned in October 1881 and many of its leaders interned. In the end, the land question in Ireland was partially solved in a reactionary way, by a deal at the top. This succeeded in defusing the issue and transferred the land back into Irish hands. In 1870 only 3 per cent of Irish farmers had owned their own land (20,000 holdings out of 680,000). By 1895 the figure was 12 per cent. In the three years after Wyndham's Act it nearly doubled, to 29 per cent; and by 1918 it had reached 64 per cent. In itself this solved nothing for the poor peasants. Irish ownership of the land and the means of production, on the basis of capitalism simply means swapping one oppressor for another as far as the Irish workers and peasants are concerned.

The combination of repression and concession carried out by the ruling class succeeded in its objective: the revolutionary agitation in the Irish countryside declined. The demise of the Land League, however, led directly to a revival of the socialist movement in Ireland. The "land war" of 1879-82 led to the politicisation of many in Ireland and in Britain. The Democratic Federation, which had formed as a result of the Irish agitation, went on to develop into Britain's first "nationwide" socialist organisation and in 1884 was renamed as the Social Democratic Federation (SDF). In 1881 the Democratic Federation was founded in Britain by radicals (and some socialists) who opposed the use of coercive legislation against the Irish Land League. This was a reflection of the fact that the bourgeois Liberals had failed to provide a solution for any of the problems of the Irish people.

Home Rule and Ulster

The attempts of Gladstone to resolve the Irish question through Home Rule were aborted by the opposition of the reactionary Tory and landowning interests, which feared that Home Rule would mean the end of their power and privileges. They made use of the Orange reactionaries to block the movement. In 1886, Lord Randolph Churchill went to Ulster, and rallied the Protestants and Presbyterians there under the slogan "Ulster will fight and Ulster will be right." In February of that year he wrote:

"I decided some time ago that if [Gladstone] went for Home Rule, the Orange card would be the one to play. Please God it may turn out to be the ace of trumps and not the deuce."

The immediate result of this manoeuvre was an outbreak of sectarian rioting in Belfast against Home Rule. The British imperialists were prepared to use sectarianism and to whip up prejudices for their own ends. But they cared little or nothing for the problems of either Protestants or Catholics, except as cannon fodder and pawns in a game. Their attitude was one of unbridled cynicism, as shown by the remark of Sir William Harncourt in a conversation with Gladstone: "The only difference is that where you can buy a Nationalist for five pounds, you must pay six pounds for a Loyalist." (Quoted in P. Johnson, op cit, p. 135.)

The House of Lords defeated the second Home Rule Bill in 1892 by the enormous majority of 419 to 41. Gladstone wanted to go to the country on the slogan "Peers versus the People" but the proposal was unceremoniously turned down by his colleagues. In this way, Home Rule was killed off for a further 15 years.

Despite this, the Irish bourgeois nationalists continued to place all their trust in the Liberals. When the latter won a landslide victory in 1906, John Redmond's Nationalists solidly backed them in parliament, although with an overall majority of 88, the Liberals had no need of them. In this atmosphere of craven capitulation, the revolutionary spirit of the Irish people was only kept alive by the working class.

In 1906 the Lords rejected the Lloyd George budget and in the elections of 1910 the Irish question once more came to the fore. The Liberal majority had shrunk to the point where they depended on the votes of the Irish MPs. Having pushed through legislation that reduced the power of the Lords, Asquith was now obliged to back a Bill for Home Rule.

At this point the Ulster question assumed a burning importance. In 1800, Belfast had a population of only 20,000 - less than one-third of Cork (70,000) and one-seventh of Dublin (172,000). By 1881 it was 186,000 and by the turn of the century 400,000. Whereas the South remained predominantly agricultural, the North had a heavy concentration of industry, including shipbuilding. The British imperialists therefore had powerful economic and also strategic reasons for holding onto the North at all costs. Thus, by stoking the fires of religious sectarianism, the imperialists were pursuing a cynical, cold and calculating self-interest.

The 1911 census (the last taken in a united Ireland) showed a total population of 4,390,219, of which Catholics made up 75 per cent, and 25 per cent were Protestants of different denominations: 576,611 Church of Ireland, 440,525 Presbyterians and 60,000 Methodists. Most of the Protestants lived in Ulster - a region originally consisting of nine counties as opposed to the artificial six county statelet given that name by British imperialism. In four counties of Ulster - Armagh, Down, Derry and Antrim - they were a large majority. But in Fermanagh and Tyrone they were a minority, although a substantial one. There were large Catholic minorities in both Derry and Belfast. And it was not possible to separate the two communities without the kind of violent ethnic cleansing we have witnessed in recent years in Yugoslavia.

In 1798, the Revolution of the United Irishmen had been enthusiastically supported by the poor Protestants. Ever since then, the imperialists had encouraged the growth of sectarianism. Originally the Orange Order was composed mainly of artisans and working class elements. Only after 1886, when Home Rule became a major issue, did the Orange Order become transformed into a weapon of reaction and a bulwark of Order, Property and Imperialism. It was in effect taken over and absorbed by the Unionist movement.

For opportunist reasons, Randolph Churchill pledged physical support from Britain to resist Home Rule - a pledge that united Ulster Unionists, Liberal Unionists and Conservative Unionists for the next thirty years. The Ulster Unionists were a mass movement based on the farmers, small businessmen and backward sections of the working class in the North. But it was led by landed aristocrats and wealthy businessmen who managed to control and manipulate the Protestant masses, playing on their fears of domination by Rome. A factor in the resistance of Protestants to Home Rule was the conduct of the Vatican, with the reactionary Pope Pius X (1903-14), who condemned "Modernism" in all forms and laid down new rules for mixed marriages which were an insult and a provocation to Protestants, playing into the hands of the bigots who argued that "Home Rule is Rome Rule".

The only hope of defeating the forces of Orange reaction was to split away the Protestant workers and small farmers from the control of the landlords and capitalists. This could only be done on a class basis. In fact, under the leadership of Connolly and Larkin, the organised working class posed a serious threat to the Orange Establishment in the period of stormy class struggles before 1914.

The Orange movement has never been homogeneous. Within it there is a sharp class division that reappears at every decisive turn and threatens to produce a split along class lines. In the period of the reawakening of the working class movement in the 1900s, pressure from the working class led to an open split in the Orange Order, as Emett Larkin explains:

"The result of this discontent was the formation of the ultra-militant Belfast Association by Arthur Trew and T.H. Sloan. The Grand Orange Lodge watched the B.P.A. [British Protestant Association] with the suspicious and waiting eye that all orthodoxies fixes on its rigorists, but it had to tread carefully because the rank and file of the Order vigorously backed Trew and his Association. *There was also an indication of a split along class lines, as the 'majority of the Grand Lodge were well-to-do merchants, Justices of the Peace, and clergymen having little to do with Trew and his supporters who were chiefly working men.*" (Emmett Larkin, James Larkin, p. 282, our emphasis.)

The Independent Orange Order

Trew was an extreme Protestant bigot who was eventually jailed for inciting violence against Catholics. But the man who replaced him, T.H. Sloan was another matter. A shipyard cement worker, Sloan contested the seat of South Belfast in 1902 as the "Democratic candidate" and defeated his Tory opponent, a wealthy landowner from County Down by 800 votes in a total poll of nearly 6,000. As a result the Grand Lodge suspended him. Several Belfast Lodges protested against this and were themselves suspended. In an act of defiance they united with other dissident Lodges to form the Independent Orange Order.

The evolution of the Independent Orange Order must be one of the strangest of history's many peculiar transformations. Under the guidance of R. Lindsay Crawford, a Dublin Orangeman and editor of *The Irish Protestant*, the Independent Orange Order broke from the old Protestant bigotry of Trew and advocated a more tolerant line on religion and even on the national question. In July 1905 the Order issued a manifesto *To all Irishmen Whose Country Stands First in their Affections* in which we read:

"The victory of our forefathers at the Boyne was not a victory over creed or over race, but a victory for human liberty, the fruits of which our Roman Catholic countrymen share no less than ourselves... As Irishmen, we do not seek to asperse the memory of the hallowed dead whose fortunes were linked with those of the ill-starred house of Stuart, and whose courage and daring were proved in many a hard-fought field. We stand once more on the banks of the Boyne, and not as victors in the fight, not to applaud the noble deeds of our ancestors, but to bridge the gulf that has so long divided Ireland into hostile camps, and to hold out the right hand of friendship to those who, whilst worshipping at other shrines, are yet our fellow-countrymen - bone of our bone and flesh of our flesh. We come to help in the Christian task of binding up the bleeding wounds of our country, and to co-operate with all who place Ireland first in their affections...

"In an Ireland in which Protestant and Roman Catholic stand sullen and discontented, it is not too much to hope that both will reconsider their positions and, in their common trials, unite on a true basis of nationality. The higher claims of our distracted country have too long been neglected in the strife of party and of creed. The man who cannot rise above the trammels of party and of sect on a national issue is a foe to nationality and to human freedom." (Quoted in Larkin, ibid, p. 236.)

Part Four

The workers' movement

In the years before the outbreak of the First World War, British imperialism was facing a revolutionary movement both in Ireland and at home. The threat came not from middle class nationalists but from the organised working class. For most of the 19th century the land question had been the central issue in Ireland. But now a new force emerged on the stage - the Irish working class. Under the leadership of James Larkin and James Connolly, the class question came to the fore. Both men were revolutionary Marxists.

Marxism is often portrayed as something alien to Ireland, a kind of foreign import. In fact, it has a long and honourable tradition in Ireland. James Connolly, was a committed and militant Marxist all his life. But as often happens in the history of revolutionaries, Connolly was attacked and slandered all his life by the bourgeoisie, but after his death he has been turned into a kind of harmless icon. People are invited to genuflect before the icon, but are actively discouraged from taking a serious interest in his ideas. One of the central ideas of Connolly which has been systematically ignored is that *the national liberation struggle is inseparable from the struggle for socialism*. What is required is a militant united front against capitalism and imperialism, which would unite all the oppressed and exploited layers of society under the leadership of the proletariat. Without this, all talk of national liberation is just so much moonshine and demagogy.

In the years before the First World War, Connolly and Larkin struggled to unite the Irish working class and build an independent labour movement. They built the Irish Transport and General Workers' Union, not merely as an organisation to fight for better wages and conditions but as a revolutionary vehicle to change society. The epic struggle of the Dublin workers in 1913 furnished ample proof of the revolutionary potential and fighting spirit of the Irish working class. For nearly six months, 20,000 men and women, on whom a further 80,000 depended for their daily bread, were locked out by the employers because they refused to sign a pledge that they would never join the union, or resign from it if they were members.

The British working class actively supported their class brothers and sisters in Ireland. The infant Labour Party in Britain supported the cause of Home Rule for Ireland, a fact that was commented on favourably by Connolly, who never saw the people of Britain as the enemy and consistently tried to establish close fraternal ties with the workers and the Labour Movement in England, Wales and Scotland.

The Irish workers' movement has an old and honourable tradition, beginning with the establishment of branches of the International Working Men's Association (or First International). In 1870, six years after its foundation, branches of the First International were formed throughout Ireland, with the main centres being, Dublin and Cork. However, because of the domination and control of the Catholic Church over working class people the International was soon suppressed. In Britain, Irish exiles were more active. A major focus of the International was the plight of the Irish political prisoners in British jails. In this respect the campaign in Ireland for the release of the Fenian Prisoners, united with the campaign already pursued by the First International. The International also recognised the Irish peoples right to self-determination.

The Dublin branch of the International first emerged in mid-February 1872 but was routed by April. All of its public meetings were under sever attack because of the killing of the Archbishop of Paris during the Paris Commune. The final meeting, held at McKeon's premises in Chapel Lane on 7th April, sealed the fate of the branch when a mob of anti-Internationalists stormed the building. According to a hostile *Irish Times*: "The defenders of the Communists of Paris were set upon, and a hand-to-hand encounter ensued.... chairs and tables were upset, the glass was smashed in the windows, and every stray piece of wood was availed of as a weapon for attack or defence....several members of the detective force were in the room at the time, but exercising a wise discretion allowed the parties to fight it out".

The meeting was broken up and the members chased down the stairs and up the street by an incensed mob. The same story was repeated elsewhere. In Cork the Internationalists had had a certain success and established links with local workers (the coach-builders). According to *The Freeman's Journal* the Cork membership reached three hundred within a few weeks of the branch's formation in late-February 1872. But then the local clergy declared them to be "against religion" and called on Cork workers to crush them.

On 24th March three thousand people turned out for a rally against the International, but the Internationalists appeared with "a body of men, perhaps about one hundred in number, composed of working men, and in parts of roughs, nearly all of whom wore green neckties". In the ensuing riot the meeting-hall was wrecked: "They rallied at both sides repeatedly, and the taking and re-taking of the platform was conducted by leaders who were armed with bludgeons.... The building was very much damaged". After several hours of rioting the Internationalists emerged victorious. Within weeks, however, a "red-scare", exacerbated by the riot, caused the branch to dissolve.

Dublin Democratic Association

After the smashing of the International, labour was dormant for a while, though there were always individuals and small groups who kept the flag flying. The main movement at that time was the Irish Land League. In January 1885 the Dublin Democratic Association was formed. Its stated objective was "to promote and defend the rights of labour, and to restore the land to the people", but it did not last long. The real beginning of modern organised socialism in Ireland was the launching of the Dublin branch of the Socialist League in December 1895. The following year this became the Irish Socialist Republican Party.

The birth of the Irish Labour movement and the development of the Labour movement in Britain were interlinked. At a time when the Labour Party was establishing itself as the party of the working class on the other side of the Irish Sea, the basis was being laid in Ireland for a genuinely Socialist Republican movement. It was James Connolly who formed the Irish Socialist Republican Party in May 1896. The ISRP, it is true, never gained much support outside Dublin and Cork, but the influence of the teachings of Connolly ensured that its ideology and objectives survived.

Connolly had a great "feel" for the mass movement and he immediately realised the importance of winning over the trade unions, which at that time were directly or indirectly under the control of the extreme right wing Nationalist Party, the Irish Parliamentary Party. These bourgeois nationalists represented the employers with the support of the Catholic Church. The prior condition for the emancipation of the working class was to establish its complete political and organisational independence from the bourgeoisie. The idea of class independence was hammered home by Connolly from the beginning to the end of his life.

The first step was to found a newspaper in order to create a political awareness and to expose the false propaganda of the capitalist media. *The Workers Republic* was launched on the 13th August 1898 as the voice of the ISRP. Kier Hardie realised the potential of the ISRP and gave a donation of fifty pounds to start the paper. *The Workers Republic* was the first Marxist paper in Ireland.

Eighty-five issues of *The Workers Republic* were published between 1898 and 1903. The paper did not survive after Connolly's departure for America in 1903. However, *The Workers Republic* became the springboard for the ISRP and the emergence of Marxism in Ireland. For the first time socialists broke through the old secretive and underground nature of Irish politics and began to integrate themselves with the masses. In all the main cities, branches of the ISRP were established.

The basic idea defended by Connolly was expressed in the title of his paper. For the first time the workers of Ireland inscribed proudly on their banner the slogan of the Republic, but added, recalling the phrase of Wolfe Tone, that what was needed was a republic of the "men (and women) of no property" - *a workers' republic*. In this way the aim of national liberation was inseparably linked to the struggle for the socialist transformation of society. All subsequent history has shown that this approach was the only correct one.

The ISRP from the outset adopted a consistent internationalist position, as shown by its stance on the Boer War. It succeeded in defeating jingoism and organising a mass protest movement against the war. One of the resolutions passed at a public meeting in College Green, then an area of the Dublin ruling class, called upon the Irish in Transvaal to take up arms against the army of British capitalism.

The ISRP under Connolly's leadership realised the potential of the masses. Public meetings were organised in protest against the Boer War, of which many thousands of people participated. The party was the main organiser of the Great Jubilee Protest of 1897, when the working class people of Dublin disrupted the Jubilee celebrations. An event on which the British establishment in Ireland had lavished many hundreds of thousands of pounds and two years of preparation was thrown into disarray. Connolly wrote a vitriolic attack upon the monarchy, British imperialism and those "Irish nationalists" who bowed before her majesty, opening his assault with his favourite quotation, from the French revolutionary Camille Desmoulins, "The great appear great to us only because we are on our knees. Let us rise!"

Unfortunately, when Connolly left for America in 1903, the Republican socialist movement fragmented. In 1908, a group of former members of the ISRP in Dublin invited Connolly back to Ireland, to help launch the new Socialist Party of Ireland, with a weekly wage of two pounds a week. When Connolly returned to Ireland, Larkin had already formed the ITGWU, which dominated the industrial and political climate. The scene was set for a stormy period of class struggle that lasted right up till the First World War.

The class struggle before WW1

In the general election of 1906, the Orange Order had a hard fight on its hands to keep control of Belfast council. William Walker, the Labour Party candidate came within 300 votes of capturing the Orange stronghold of North Belfast. The

...ary F.H. Crawford moaned: "We have lost a lot of the staunch ...men in Belfast. They consider themselves betrayed by their leader ... Balfour and they have gone for the Labour and socialist programmes. This is what we have to combat locally. The old Unionist enthusiasm is dead among the masses here. These are facts and all in touch with the working men know it."

The reason for this transformation was a sharp upturn in the class struggle, which always cuts across the poison of chauvinism, racism and sectarianism. R.M. Fox describes the revolutionary scenes in Belfast in 1907 when one section of workers after another staged stormy strikes, in which the Protestant working class played a militant role:

"Mr. James MacDonald, manager of the Belfast Steamship Company, requested a head constable to remove the crowd clustering at the quayside. This he declined to do. District Inspector Dunlop was then asked to intervene and, on his orders, the crowd was pushed back. There was a growing disorder. Sometime in the afternoon a striker appeared with a Union Jack inscribed, 'Down with the Blacklegs'. This was a centre of turmoil." (R.M. Fox, *James Larkin, Irish Labour Leader*, p. 33.)

The employers, in customary fashion, tried to split the workers along sectarian lines. Using the occasion of the Orange parades of 12th July, the coal merchants closed the yards:

"The coal workers were renowned for their toughness. And the merchants probably reckoned on clashes between Protestant and Catholic groups when thousands of idle men were flung on the streets on this day, traditionally given over to sectarian combat. The papers had denounced Larkin as a Nationalist troublemaker and had prepared the ground well. It was a shrewd calculation that when the Orange processions streamed up with their drums and banners, workers would split into Orange and Green camps. This had always happened before. But this time Larkin had posters up all over the city appealing to the workers to come to a great demonstration at the Customs House Steps, not as Catholics or as Protestants, but as workers determined to enforce their economic demands. He marched at the head of a gigantic labour procession in which Orange and Green bands both took part. This was a new era, a lasting sensation. People rubbed their eyes and wondered. It was agreed that only Larkin could bring these contending factions together and infuse them with a single purpose. Larkin had been blackened in the Unionist press. It was widely said that he was only using Labour to advance his subversive Nationalist aims. The July 12th demonstration blew all this disunity propaganda sky high. To emphasise the general feeling, the Independent Orange Order, at a separate meeting, collected £50 for the strikers." (R.M. Fox, ibid, pp. 44-5.)

Under such conditions the bigots and sectarians were powerless to split the movement. One strike followed another, and the class instincts of the workers predominated over all else. There were strikes of the Belfast dockers, carters and coalmen. Such was the charged atmosphere that even the Royal Irish Constabulary in Belfast mutinied over pay and its members had to be transferred to remote country districts. When the employers tried to whip up sectarianism to divide the workers, the union replied with a handbill reading "Not as Catholics or Protestants, as Nationalists or Unionists, but as Belfast men and workers, stand together and don't be misled by the employers' game of dividing Catholic and Protestant." (Larkin, op cit, p. 31.)

The role of the leadership - in this case Larkin - played a decisive role in uniting the workers. But the main point to understand is that the class struggle always tends to cut across all divisions in the working class, whether of language, religion, nationality, sex or race. Unity is the main weapon of the working class. To build unity, to eliminate division, to wield the class together in struggle against the common enemy - that is the principle duty of all who aspire to a better life. On the other hand, to divide the working class is the main task of reactionaries of all kinds. Once the class is united and mobilised in struggle, it will sweep aside all sectarian divisions as a man sweeps aside a gnat with a brush of the hand. But this can only be achieved by concentrating unswervingly on the *class* issues. This is what Larkin and Connolly did and they succeeded brilliantly. That is the lesson we must learn, and these are the methods we must strive to imitate.

Carson organises the reaction

While the moderate bourgeois Nationalists placed all their hopes on parliamentary activity and deals with the British Liberals, the forces of reaction were organising and arming outside parliament. That was quite natural. All history shows the limitation of parliamentary activity. Marxists are in favour of making full use of parliament for furthering the cause of the working class. We will make use of each and every legal opportunity that is available to us, but we are also realists and we understand that no ruling class in history has ever given up its power and privileges without a fight with no holds barred.

In the last analysis, all decisive questions are settled outside parliament, by the struggle of opposing class forces. What happened in the period before 1914 is a very graphic illustration of this fact. The "democratic" landlords and capitalists of the North of Ireland did not hesitate to organise armed resistance to the legally elected government in London as soon as their interests were threatened. And they immediately got the support of the British Conservative Party and the tops of the British army, who rebelled against the Constitution and refused to obey orders. They put solidarity with their class brothers before all laws, constitutions, rules and regulations - and they won. There are many lessons in this.

The passing of the 1911 Parliament Act, which was intended to limit the powers of the House of Lords to block the Third Home Rule Bill, was the signal for the mobilisation of the Orange reaction. In September Lord Carson told a parade of 50,000 men:

"We must be prepared, in the possible event of a Home Rule Bill passing, with such measures as will carry on for ourselves the government of those districts of which we have control. We must be prepared... the morning Home Rule passes, ourselves to become responsible for the Government of the Protestant Province of Ulster (*cheers*)." (P. Johnson, op cit, p. 164.)

The only force capable of defeating the reactionaries was the working class on both sides of the Irish Sea. Only united working class action could have undermined Carson's reactionary movement by driving a wedge between working class Protestants and the Carsonite leaders of the Orange Order. In the summer of 1911, the class struggle was in full swing in Britain and Ireland. In Britain there were two great national strikes - of the railway and transport workers, followed by strikes of the seamen, firemen, dockers, coal-fillers and carters. The Dublin dockers refused to unload ships from striking ports in Britain and Irish railway workers loyally supported the strike of their British comrades, who in return supported the Irish workers with money and food during the Dublin lockout.

Connolly was, first and foremost, a militant workers' leader and a revolutionary socialist. The Irish Transport and General Workers' Union (ITGWU), under the leadership of Larkin and Connolly, led the stormy wave of class struggle that shook Ireland to its foundations in the years before 1914. Rarely have these Islands seen such a level of bitter class conflict. This affected not only Dublin but also Belfast, where Connolly succeeded in uniting Catholic and Protestant workers in struggle against the employers. In October 1911 he led the famous Belfast Textile workers' strike and organised the workers of that sector - predominately low-paid and very exploited women.

The Dublin Lockout

The wave of strikes was countered by the employers in the notorious Dublin lockout of 1913, affecting 25,000 workers by September. Here we saw the real face of the Irish bourgeoisie: grasping, repressive, reactionary. The Dublin bosses, organised by William Martin Murphy, the chairman of the Employers' Federation and owner of the *Irish Independent* newspaper, set out to crush the workers and their organisations. The ITGWU replied by blacking Murphy's newspapers, and he retaliated by locking out all union members. Those locked-out were given a letter to sign, stating that they would have nothing to do with

Larkin's union.

Here once more we see how class considerations weighed more heavily than anything else. The Irish bourgeois Nationalists led by John Redmond backed the employers in the lockout. Their paper the *Freeman's Journal* railed against "syndicalism" in its editorials. *For his part, Connolly urged the workers to vote Labour, even if it meant endangering the Home Rule Bill being put forward by the Liberals with the support of the Irish bourgeois Nationalists.* This shows that Connolly put the class interests of the workers before all else, and refused to subordinate the class struggle to the siren appeals for "national unity". For Connolly, the "labour question" was *always* primary. Following in the steps of Wolfe Tone, he understood that only the working people - the "men (and women) of no property" - could solve the national question. And all later history shows that he was right.

Connolly was shown to be right to distrust the British Liberals and their Irish nationalist stooges. Although the government was threatened by Carson, the Liberals took no action against him, while arresting and sentencing Larkin to hard labour on a charge of seditious libel. The representatives of the propertied classes on both sides of the Irish Sea knew who their main enemies were. The issue of *class unity* runs like a red thread through all the writings and speeches of Connolly: "Perhaps they will see that the landlord who grinds his peasants on a Connemara estate, and the landlord who rack-rents them in a Cowgate slum, are brethren in fact and deed. Perhaps they will realise that the Irish worker who starves in an Irish cabin and the Scots worker who is poisoned in an Edinburgh garret are brothers with one hope and destiny." (C.D. Greaves, *James Connolly*, p. 61.)

Throughout the lockout, Larkin and Connolly repeatedly appealed to the class solidarity of the British workers. They addressed mass rallies in England, Scotland and Wales, which were also the scene of big class battles in the years before the war. The appeal of the Irish workers did not fall on deaf ears. Their cause was enthusiastically supported by the rank and file of the British movement, although the right-wing Labour leaders were preparing to ditch the Irish workers as soon as the opportunity presented itself. Despite the solidarity and sympathy of the workers of Britain, the trade union leaders refused to organise solidarity strikes, the only way that victory could have been achieved.

The Irish bourgeois nationalists played a shameful role. Arthur Griffith poured scorn on the solidarity of the Irish and British workers: "It has recently been discovered", he sneered, "that the Irish working man is not an Irish working man at all. He is a unit of humanity, a human label of internationalism, a brother of the men over the water who rule his country." Of course, the workers of England, Wales and Scotland did not even rule their own country, let alone Ireland. The class sympathy and solidarity of the British workers with their Irish brothers and sisters was as natural as that between Arthur Griffith and the Irish bosses who were starving their "fellow Irish" into submission.

The Catholic Church played an even more shameful role, encouraging sectarianism in order to divide the workers and undermine them. Above all, it strove to break the links between Irish and British workers. When the workers of Liverpool and Glasgow invited the starving children of locked-out workers in Dublin to their homes, the priests whipped up a hysterical campaign against Catholic children being shipped off to the homes of the "ungodly" English. Better they should starve than to accept the bread of Protestants! In the end, their wish was granted. The Irish workers were starved back to work. Bitterly, Connolly noted:

"And so we Irish workers must again go down to Hell, bow our backs to the last of the slave drivers, let our hearts be seared by the iron of his hatred and instead of the sacramental wafer of brotherhood and common sacrifice, eat the dust of defeat and betrayal. Dublin is isolated." (*Forward*, February 9, 1914)

The Citizen's Army

In the years preceding World War One, the ruling class was facing revolutionary developments in Ireland and in Britain. Between 1907 and 1912 the graph of the strike movement rose steadily: the number of days lost in strikes increased from 1,878,679 to 38,142,101. Under the pressure of the working class and the rise of the Labour Party, the Liberals were compelled to make concessions, including an increase in democratic rights. In 1911 the powers of the House of Lords were limited by an Act of Parliament that reduced its ability to block legislation from the lower house. The Lords could delay the passing of a law for three times in one parliamentary session, but no more. In this way, the road was open for the approval of Irish Home Rule.

But all history shows that the ruling class is prepared to resort to extra-parliamentary measures when its vital interests are threatened. In order to head off the danger of Home Rule, the most reactionary circles in Britain and Ireland resorted once more to the "Orange card". Lord Carson organised and armed the hooligans of the Belfast slums in the Ulster Volunteers, with 100,000 armed members, pledged to resist Irish Home Rule by force. When the Liberal government in London made a half-hearted attempt to disarm them using the British Army in Ireland, they were met with the mutiny of British army officers at the Curragh, supported by the Tory Party.

When their interests were threatened, the reactionaries simply tore up the laws of the land and came out onto the streets, and the working class prepared to confront them. Carson whipped up an orgy of sectarian violence in Belfast. The

Liberal government, which did not hesitate to send troops to South Wales to fire on striking workers, did nothing to deal with the mutiny at the Curragh or to halt the pogroms against Catholics in Belfast. Connolly remained firm in the face of the sectarian madness. He organised a Labour demonstration under the auspices of the ITGWU, "the only union that allows no bigotry in its ranks." In answer to the sectarians and religious bigots, he declared *class war*, issuing his famous manifesto: *To the Linen Slaves of Belfast.*

In 1913, as an answer to the threat of force from the counterrevolution, the Irish workers organised the Citizens' Army - the first Red Army in the world. *This was a working class militia based on the trade unions.* In order to protect themselves against the brutal attacks of police and hired thugs of the employers, the workers set up their own defence force: the Irish Citizens' Army (ICA). This was the first time in these Islands that workers had organised themselves on an armed basis to defend themselves against the common enemy: the bosses and the scabs. The latter, it should be remembered, were much more numerous than at the present time, as a result of the widespread conditions of poverty and despair.

The Irish Labour and trade union movement adopted a firm class stand. The Irish Trade Union Congress Parliamentary Committee issued a *Manifesto to the Workers of Ireland* that stated:

"As Irish workers we are not concerned with the officers of the British Army taking the line they have nor are we concerned because of the effects their action may have upon Britain's Army; but we claim that what the officer may do in pursuance of his political and sectarian convictions, so, too, may the private in pursuance of his; and if today British Generals and other Staff Officers refuse to fight against the privileged class to which they belong so, too, must the Private Soldier be allowed to exercise his convictions against shooting down his brothers and sisters of the working class when they are fighting for their rights...." (Clifford King, *The Orange and the Green*, p. 36.)

The Parliamentary Committee of the Irish TUC remarked: "that in strongly and emphatically protesting against the recent attempt of certain army officers to utilise the armed forces in this country for the purpose of furthering the interests of their class, we desire to impress on the workers the necessity for learning aright and fully digesting the full significance of this action, and in future apply it in a similar manner in the interests of their own class." (Larkin, op. cit., pp. 160-1.)

Just such an application of those lessons was the establishment of the Irish Citizens' Army. The two main leaders of the ICA were Connolly (himself an ex-soldier) and Captain Jack J. White, D.S.O. - a Protestant Ulsterman. Connolly saw the ICA not only as a defence force, but as a revolutionary army, dedicated to the overthrow of capitalism and imperialism. He wrote:

"An armed organisation of the Irish working class is a phenomenon in Ireland.

Hitherto, the workers of Ireland have fought as parts of the armies led by their masters, never as a member of any army officered, trained, and inspired by men of their own class. Now, with arms in their hands, they propose to steer their own course, to carve their own future." (*The Workers Republic*, 30th October 1915.)

As we see from these lines, Connolly envisaged the ICA in class terms, as an organisation organically linked to the mass organisations of the proletariat. It was funded out of the subscriptions of the members of the union, and its activities were organised from Liberty Hall, the headquarters of the ITGWU in Dublin. The Citizens Army drilled and paraded openly on the streets of Dublin for several years before 1916. Here was no secret organisation engaged in the methods of individual terrorism, but a genuine workers' militia: the first workers' Red Army in Europe.

Part Five

The Easter Rising

The years preceding the First World War witnessed a period of bitter class struggle in Ireland, with stormy strikes and lock-outs being fought out against the background of the national struggle for the liberation of Ireland from English rule. By 1914, Ireland stood on the brink of civil war. Unfortunately, the strike movement in Ireland was rudely cut across by the outbreak of the war between Britain and Germany. Yet on the other hand the outbreak of the First World War brought all the contradictions arising from the national question to boiling point.

In the First World War, Connolly pursued *a consistently internationalist line*. Although he had no direct contact with Lenin, the two men instinctively adopted the same position from the outbreak of hostilities. Meanwhile the leadership of most of the European Labour movement took a chauvinist position, that is to say, despite all their espoused opposition to war before it began, once it was underway they supported "their own" ruling class. Larkin, like Connolly, took the opposite starting point, that is, they supported the interests of the international working class: "I have been accused of being pro-German, but I am not for the Kaiser any more than I am for George Wettin of England. I am for the working classes of every country. The English working class is as dear to me as that of my own country or any other, but the government of England is the vilest thing on the face of the earth." (Larkin, op. cit., p. 172.)

In August 1914, despite all the resolutions passed by the congresses of the Socialist International, every one of the leaderships of the Social Democratic Parties betrayed the cause of socialist internationalism and voted for the War. The only honourable exceptions were the Russians, the Serbs - and the Irish. Right from the start, Connolly adopted an unswerving internationalist stance. Commenting on the betrayal of the leaders of the Socialist International, he wrote in *Forward* (15th August, 1914):

"What then becomes of all our resolutions; all our protests of fraternisation; all our threats of general strikes; all our carefully built machinery of internationalism; all our hopes for the future?"

In answer to the kind of pacifism that was the hallmark of Labour Lefts such as Ramsay MacDonald (at that time on the left of the British Labour movement) and the leaders of the ILP, he wrote:

"A great continental uprising of the working class would stop the war; a universal protest at public meetings would not save a single life from being wantonly slaughtered."

These lines show that James Connolly was a genuine proletarian and revolutionary who dedicated all his life to the cause of the working class and socialism. Connolly was not just a socialist, not just a revolutionary: *he was an internationalist to the marrow of his bones.* The programme of the Irish Socialist Republican Party, written by Connolly, was not a nationalist but a socialist programme based upon:

"Establishment of an *Irish Socialist Republic* based on the public ownership by the Irish people of the land, and instruments of production, distribution and exchange. Agriculture to be administered as a public function, under boards of management elected by the agricultural population and responsible to them and to the nation at large. All other forms of labour necessary to the well-being of the community to be conducted on the same principles."

The uncompromising socialism of the ISRP went hand in hand with revolutionary proletarian internationalism. Larkin explained: "my object was to see a deadlock arrived at, hoping that the workers would revolt in several countries." (Ibid. pp. 173-4.) Connolly wrote and spoke on the same lines. It was the elementary duty of the Irish working class to take advantage of the situation to wage a revolutionary struggle against British imperialism, on the assumption that "England's need is Ireland's opportunity". Unfortunately, the Irish workers were exhausted by the exertions of the class battles before the war, and the revolutionary wave would only begin in 1917. In the first years of the war, the workers' movement was silent.

The problem was that from the start of the War, Connolly was virtually isolated. Internationally, he had no contact. Outside of Ireland, the Labour movement seemed to be as silent as the grave. True, there were symptoms of a revival in Britain, with the Glasgow rent strike of 1915 and the rise of the rank-and-file shop stewards movement. But Connolly feared that the workers of Britain would move too late, and that Ireland could not wait. Matters came to a head over the question of military conscription.

The idea of an uprising had clearly been taking shape in Connolly's mind. The threat that Britain would introduce conscription into Ireland was the main issue that concentrated the mind, not only of Connolly, but also of the petit bourgeois nationalists of the Irish Volunteers. Connolly therefore pressed them to enter a militant alliance with Labour for an armed uprising against British imperialism. In the event, the leaders of the Volunteers withdrew at the last movement, leaving the Rising in the lurch.

Nationalists betray

For generations the Irish nationalists have assiduously built up a mythology around the Easter Rising. However, what is never truthfully explained by them is the class forces that were involved. The role of the Citizens' Army has never been fairly portrayed in any of their histories. Nor is the fact that the middle class nationalists betrayed the Easter Rising. *In reality the driving force for the uprising was the Irish working class, fighting not just for Irish independence, but for the Irish Workers' Republic.* The units of the Citizens' Army were the hard core of the uprising. And at its head stood that great leader and martyr of the working class, James Connolly.

Lenin explained that in a united front the correct tactic is to "march separately and strike together." Although they collaborated in the Rising, there was always a conflict between the workers of the Citizens' Army and the middle class nationalist leadership of the Irish Volunteers. Connolly's identification with the 1916 Rising was a clear-cut recognition of the connection and the links between the national struggle and the class struggle. Connolly identified himself completely with the Rising. He led the Rising in Dublin city. But he had to accept as allies the Irish Volunteers, led by Eoin MacNeil who was a died-in-the-wool reactionary nationalist. As a revolutionary and internationalist, Connolly was naturally in favour of fighting against the British rule in Ireland. But he warned the Irish workers a thousand times not to be fooled by the bourgeois and petty bourgeois nationalists and their demagogy about "freeing Ireland" under capitalist rule.

The spark that ignited the revolt was the plan to introduce military conscription in Ireland - to force the youth of Ireland to act as cannon fodder for their imperial masters. *Yet the right wing Irish nationalists actually supported British imperialism, acting as its recruiting sergeants in the War.* Connolly savaged them for sending the flower of Ireland's youth to die for imperialism in the trenches. With scathing wit he wrote:

"Full steam ahead, John Redmond said, that everything was well chum,
Home Rule will come, when we are dead and buried out in Belgium."

Even the supposedly progressive wing of the Nationalists sabotaged the movement by countermanding the order to mobilise on the eve of the uprising. Only

1,500 members of the Dublin Volunteers and ICA answered the call to rise. The nationalists had already split between the Redmondites - the Parliamentary Irish Group - who backed the War, and the left wing. *However, on the eve of the Rising, the leader of the Volunteers, Eoin MacNeil publicly instructed all members to refuse to come out. The Irish bosses were unanimous in denouncing the Rising. Arthur Griffith described it as "lunacy". As so many times before and since, the nationalist bourgeoisie betrayed the cause of Ireland.*

From a military point of view the Rising was doomed in advance - although if the Volunteers had not stabbed it in the back, the uprising could have had far greater success. It was virtually confined to Dublin, where only about a thousand fighters took part in it. Liam Mellows led a similar number of insurgents in Galway, and there was a smaller movement in Wexford, but elsewhere the country was peaceful. The conditions for the Rising were frankly unfavourable. Although there were strikes in Ireland right up to the outbreak of the Rising, the movement was in a downswing. The Irish working class had been exhausted and weakened by the exertions of the lockout, and they remained essentially passive during the Rising.

The British forces waged a ferocious counter-offensive to crush the Rising. They used artillery to batter the GPO (the rebel centre) into submission. By Thursday night, after four days of heroic resistance against the most frightful odds, the rebels were compelled to sign an unconditional surrender. The British imperialists immediately showed their real face when they executed Connolly and the other leaders of the Rising in cold blood.

It is necessary to draw a sober-minded balance sheet of 1916. Was Connolly right to move when he did? The question is a difficult one. To some extent, the hand of the rebels was forced by events, by the introduction of conscription. There were rumours that the British authorities were planning to arrest the leading Irish revolutionaries.

Connolly seems to have decided to throw everything into the balance. He drew the conclusion that it was better to strike first. He aimed to strike a blow that would break the ice and show the way, even at the cost of his own life. To fight and lose was preferable than to accept and capitulate without a struggle. When Connolly left the HQ of the ITGWU that fateful morning, he whispered to his comrade William O'Brien: "We are going out to be slaughtered." O'Brien asked: "Is there no chance of success?" Connolly replied: "None whatever". *Connolly knew that the rising was doomed. His aim was to leave behind a tradition of revolutionary struggle upon which the new generation could build.*

Connolly was undoubtedly a giant. His actions were those of a genuine revolutionary, unlike the craven conduct of the Labour leaders who backed the imperialist slaughter - with the enthusiastic support of the Irish bourgeois nationalists. Yet he also made some mistakes. There is no point in denying it, although some people wish to make Connolly into a saint, while simultaneously ditching or distorting his ideas. There were serious weaknesses in the Rising itself. No attempt was made to call a general strike. This would have had to have been prepared in advance. On Monday 24th April, 1916, the Dublin trams were still running, and most people went about their business. No appeal was made to the British soldiers.

Thousand to one odds

The behaviour of the nationalist leaders came as no surprise to Connolly, who always approached the national liberation struggle from a class point of view. He never had any trust in the bourgeois and petit bourgeois tendencies in Republicanism, and tirelessly worked to build an independent movement of the working class as the only guarantee for the re-conquest of Ireland. Since his death there have been many attempts to erase his real identity as a revolutionary socialist and present him as just one more nationalist. This is utterly false. One week before the Rising he warned the Citizens Army: "The odds against us are a thousand to one. But if we should win, hold onto your rifles because the Volunteers may have a different goal. Remember, we are not only for political liberty, but for economic liberty as well."

Although the Rising itself ended in failure, it left behind a tradition of struggle that had far-reaching consequences. It was this that Connolly probably had in mind. In particular the savagery of the British army, which shot all the leaders of the Rising in cold blood after a farcical drumhead "trial", caused a wave of revulsion throughout all Ireland. James Connolly, who was badly wounded and unable to stand, was shot strapped to a chair. But the British had miscalculated. The gunshots that ended the life of this great leader of the working class aroused a new generation of fighters eager to revenge Ireland's wrongs.

Some sorry ex-Marxists criticised the Easter Rising from a right-wing standpoint, such as Plekhanov. In an article in *Nashe Slovo* dated 4th July 1916, Trotsky denounced Plekhanov's remarks about the Rising as "wretched and shameful" and added: "the experience of the Irish national uprising is over [....] the historical role of the Irish proletariat is just beginning."

The Easter Rising was like a tocsin bell, the echoes of which rang throughout Europe. After two years of imperialist slaughter, at last the ice was broken! A courageous word had been spoken, and could be heard above the din of the bombs and cannon-fire. Lenin received the news of the uprising enthusiastically. This was understandable, given his position. The War posed tremendous difficulties for the Marxist internationalists. Lenin was isolated with a small group of supporters.

On all sides there was capitulation and betrayal. The class struggle was temporarily in abeyance. The Labour leaders were participating in coalition governments with the social-patriots. The events in Dublin completely cut across this. That is why Lenin was so enthusiastic about the uprising. But he also pointed out:

"The misfortune of the Irish is that they have risen prematurely when the European revolt of the proletariat has not yet matured. Capitalism is not so harmoniously built that the various springs of rebellion can of themselves merge at one effort without reverses and defeats."

There is a myth that Lenin and Trotsky did not support the Rising. These lines can hopefully nail this lie. They analysed the Rising and criticized it from certain angles, but denounced all those in the international labour movement who sought to condemn this heroic episode.

The tragedy of the Easter Rising was that it occurred too soon. One year later the world was shaken by the October Revolution in Russia. Had the Rising occurred a couple of years later, it would not have been isolated. It would have had powerful reserves in the shape of the mass revolutionary movement that swept through Europe after the October Revolution in 1917. But how could Connolly have known this? He could not, and even if he had, revolutionary events cannot simply be made to fit into a neat timetable.

Betrayal of the bourgeoisie

The leading role in the Easter Rising was played by Connolly and the Citizens Army. For that reason their losses were proportionately greater. The brutal execution of Connolly in particular dealt the revolutionary movement a fatal blow. Clifford King correctly points out that "the proletariat of Dublin and the country people and peasants in the rest of the country, who warmed to the Easter leaders after they were dead, were for far too long, and for unworthy reasons, to go on being denied effective political leadership." (Clifford King, op cit, p. 36.)

Despite the fact that they played the leading role in the Rising, the history books have systematically played down the role of Connolly and the workers' Citizens' Army in 1916 and exaggerated the role of the petty bourgeois Irish volunteers and Sinn Féin. This is a travesty of the facts. Sinn Féin was an anti-socialist and anti-working class organisation. In early 1918, Larkin wrote about their American organisation thus:

"The Sinn Féin movement here is anti-labour and as for the Socialists they think they are anti-Christs. They have tried to impress the American public that the Revolution was a Catholic revolution, in fact they have done the cause the most incalculable harm. They are the most violent American jingoes, always boasting how loyal they are too and how many Irish have fought and died for this free Republic. Moroyah! They make me sick to the soul. They held a meeting in

Chicago sometime back and spent 2,600 dollars on the meeting, 1,700 dollars to erect a special star spangled flag, electrically arrayed which flashed all through the meeting. They are in a word super-fine patriots and the most consummate tricksters of politicians. This applies to all of them without exception and the crowd that have lately come over are no better." (Larkin, op. cit., p. 199.)

The Irish working class could and should have played a leading role in the national liberation struggle. This is the only way that the struggle can succeed. After 1916, the trade unions had been disorganised, but when the leaders returned from internment camps, they soon recovered. Emmet Larkin writes:

"After their release from a British internment camp in the fall of 1916, Foran and O'Brien applied themselves to their broken machine, the Transport Union. In a little over a year they had increased the membership from 5,000 to 14,000 and the branches from 10 to 40. During 1918 the growth of the Union was phenomenal, mainly because of general wage demand movement throughout Britain and Ireland. By the end of the year the membership numbered nearly 68,000 in 210 branches, and the treasury boasted a credit balance of some £19,000. When Larkin returned in April 1923, the Union totalled 100,000 members in 350 branches with a balance of £140,000." (Emmett Larkin, op. cit., p. 236).

The principal weakness of the Labour movement was its *leadership*. James Connolly was always a consistent revolutionary Marxist. He devoted a great deal of time to theory as shown by his marvellous writings. But the truth is that the other leaders of the ITGWU had no interest in theory and little understanding of socialism. They were mainly *"practicos"* for whom the trade unions were vehicles for obtaining wage increases and better conditions, not the revolutionary overthrow of capitalism. William O'Brien was typical of this type. A solid trade unionist, he had been close to Connolly, but he understood nothing of Connolly's ideas. As long as Connolly was alive, people like O'Brien were content to follow him and accept his line, although in their hearts they had grave doubts. R.M. Fox recalled that "even in Connolly's time, there was strong opposition to the Citizens' Army using the hall [Liberty Hall] and to the association of the Army with Union activities." (R.M. Fox, *History of the Citizens' Army*, p. 189.)

After Connolly's untimely death, the reformist tendencies that had always been present came to the fore. O'Brien and the other leaders, who had never been comfortable with Connolly's revolutionary line, began to distance themselves from it. They effectively renounced any independent role for Labour in the national liberation struggle, and thus handed all the initiative over to Sinn Féin and the bourgeois and petty bourgeois nationalists. When Frank Robbins, an ICA and ITGWU militant who had participated in the Easter Rising and suffered imprisonment and exile in America, returned to Ireland, he was shocked by the change. He detected "a new atmosphere, a new outlook, entirely different from that which had been moulded by Connolly and Mallin." He thought the new recruits to the ICA "seemed to lack the spirit, the understanding and the discipline which were so characteristic of the earlier period."

Robbins complained that the "close co-operation between the Irish Transport Union and the Citizens' Army seemed to have disappeared completely. Relations had indeed deteriorated to such a degree that it would not be an exaggeration to say that but for stalwarts such as I have named, an openly hostile situation would have been inevitable." (Quoted by W.K. Anderson in *James Connolly and the Irish Left*, p. 139.)

Class Independence

Larkin was very worried about the fact that after Connolly's death the Irish Labour leaders were handing over control to the Nationalists and protested about it in an angry letter to Thomas Foran, the General President of the Irish Transport and General Workers' Union in the summer of 1918: "What are O' Brien and the rest doing in allowing the Griffith gang to monopolise all the credit for the efforts? I wish O' Brien and the others would declare themselves. Are they all turned Sinn Féin?" (Larkin, op cit., p. 200.) At the end of 1918 he wrote again, urging that Irish labour must retain its class independence:

"Don't be led astray by the ephemeral political movements of a moment. Our work is fundamental. Not only do we want an independent Ireland, but we demand a free Ireland of free men and women. I realise the tortuous path you and your colleagues must walk. Certain forces in Eire seem to have exploited the struggle for their own ends. Don't be in any way deterred: hew straight to the line, let the chips fall where they may. Be assured we are on the side that must ultimately prevail. Leaders, moryah! And parties raise up and pass away in a night but men live forever and principles are permanent." (Larkin, ibid.)

However, by removing himself to the USA, Larkin had lost the chance he might have had to change the position. With Connolly gone, there was no leader with sufficient authority to put the Irish workers' movement on the right road. The workers' movement could and should have played a decisive role in the struggle but was paralysed at every decisive turn by the lack of leadership.

Frank Robbins noted bitterly:

"The failure of the Citizens' Army to play a worthwhile role in the fight against the British forces during the period of 1918-21 was due in the main to our failure to throw up leaders with dynamic vision of Connolly and Mallin. This failure was indeed a costly one for those of us who accepted the socialist principles of the workers' republic preached by James Connolly, for it meant that we missed a unique opportunity to play our part in the struggle for Irish Freedom and in the subsequent shaping of a free Ireland." (Quoted by W.K. Anderson, op cit, p. 141.)

Frank Robbins was, however, mistaken in thinking that the movement can "throw up" such a leadership. It must be built and prepared in advance, as for example, the Russian Bolshevik Party was built and prepared over a period of decades before 1917. Connolly did not build a revolutionary Marxist party - a cadre party armed with theory - which would have carried on his work after his death. Ultimately this was his biggest mistake, and one that had the most tragic consequences.

True, Connolly had created the Irish Labour Party, with a solid base in the trade unions and the working class. But it was not a cadre party and had no serious grounding in Marxist theory. This was its Achilles' heel. In effect, it was the workers of the Irish Citizens Army who had led the Easter Rising, not the petit bourgeois Volunteers. In fact, Sinn Féin played *no* role in the uprising, while the Irish bourgeois nationalists openly betrayed it. *Yet, when Connolly was removed from the picture, it was the bourgeois and petit bourgeois nationalists who took advantage of the situation to seize control of the movement.*

The leaders of the Irish Labour Party, lacking Connolly's grounding in Marxism, proved to be hopelessly inadequate to the tasks posed by history. Instead of maintaining Connolly's fight for an independent class policy, they tail ended the nationalists, scandalously standing down in their favour in the general election after the War. In the same way that the murder of Rosa Luxemburg and Karl Liebknecht later beheaded the German revolution, so the killing of Connolly removed any chance of the Irish working class leading the revolutionary movement against British imperialism. This was a heavy price to pay!

Part Six

Guerrilla war

In November 1918, having won a sweeping victory in the general elections, Sinn Féin declared for an Irish republic. This led to a national liberation struggle. The Auxiliaries - ex-officers of the British Army - acted as the shock troops of British imperialism in this war. Their leader, General Crozier, had recently returned from fighting the Bolsheviks in Russia. This was an extension of the same international class struggle.

A guerrilla war followed for three-and-a-half years, until Lloyd George agreed to negotiate the "Irish question". But the cause of national liberation was betrayed once again by the Irish bourgeois Nationalists who accepted a sell-out deal that renounced the Republic and handed the North to British imperialism. *The Irish bourgeoisie proved in practice that it was unfit to lead the national liberation struggle. The so-called Irish Free State was just a semi-colony of the British Empire, and the Irish bourgeoisie was quite happy to accept this state of affairs.* The deal split the Dail, the Army and the Irish people and prepared the ground for a bloody and ruinous civil war.

Under the leadership of the bourgeois and petit bourgeois nationalists, the movement was side-tracked into a guerrilla struggle, and then betrayed. Fearful of the prospect of revolution, the rotten Irish bourgeoisie reached an agreement with London to divide the living body of Ireland. This had been the plan "B" of British imperialism all along. Connolly had warned against this for years:

"The recent proposals of Messrs. Asquith, Devlin, Redmond and co. for the settlement of the Home Rule question deserve the earnest attention of the working class democracy of this country. They reveal in a most striking and unmistakable manner the depths of betrayal to which the so-called Nationalist politicians are willing to sink...

"Such a scheme as that agreed to by Redmond and Devlin, the betrayal of the national democracy of industrial Ulster would mean a carnival of reaction both North and South, would set back the wheels of progress, would destroy the oncoming unity of the Irish labour movement and paralyse all advanced movements whilst it endured."

All Connolly's warnings about the treacherous role of the bourgeoisie were confirmed by the terrible events surrounding partition. The legacy of this betrayal is still with us today.

"Labour must wait"

The history of Ireland for centuries has been the history of the struggle of the workers, peasants and artisans to free themselves, and of the constant shameful betrayals of the masses by their middle class and bourgeois leaders who have led the movement from defeat to defeat. It was this realisation that led Wolfe Tone to turn his attention to the "men of no property". A century later James Connolly placed this idea on a more solid footing when he argued, "Only the Irish working class remain as the incorruptible inheritors of the fight for freedom in Ireland." The bourgeoisie, for all its nationalist colouration, could not play a progressive role. The task of securing Ireland's freedom from imperialist domination now became incorporated into the tasks of the socialist revolution to be led by the working class. In freeing themselves from British imperialism the Irish working class will hardly place their necks voluntarily into the yoke of Irish capital, but march on to the Workers' Republic and the socialist transformation of society. It follows then that the central problem for both the national liberation struggle and the socialist revolution which are now welded together, is the need for the building of a genuine revolutionary party.

We have stated that the failure to build such a party was undoubtedly Connolly's most serious mistake. Although he had started out with the idea of building the Irish Socialist Republican Party (ISRP), his attention was later concentrated on the ITGWU, the Citizens' Army and the Labour Party. The goal of building a revolutionary Marxist cadre party was lost sight of. So that when Connolly was no longer present, there was nobody to take his place.

It was undoubtedly correct to fight for the establishment of an independent Labour Party based on the unions. But what was necessary was to create a disciplined Marxist tendency inside the Labour Party, fighting for a genuine Marxist programme and policy. This was not done and the Irish workers paid a terrible price for it. The tragic events after the defeat of the Easter Rising show the decisive role of leadership in the revolution. After Connolly was removed from the scene, as we have seen, the leaders of the Labour Party moved in a reformist direction. They did not play an independent role but subordinated themselves to the nationalists. This was a fatal mistake and in flat contradiction to the policy of

Connolly of uncompromising class independence. The working class lost the possibility of playing the leading role in the national struggle. The hegemony of the movement fell into the hands of bourgeois and petty bourgeois nationalists, although they never earned it. Such a leadership, as the history of Ireland amply testifies, dooms the movement to defeat and betrayal in advance.

The Irish working class showed its potential in the general strike of 1918, which was rock-solid in all Ireland. The working class came into collision with the Irish bourgeoisie from the very beginning, as shown by the stormy increase of the trade unions, strikes, land seizures and the formation of industrial and agricultural soviets. The movement was particularly advanced in the South West. There were land seizures in County Clare, where soviets were established. The miners took over the Arigna coal mine in County Leitrim. In 1919 the workers of Limerick set up a soviet that took control of the city. The following year the Dublin workers refused to unload a cargo of munitions sent from England and the railway workers refused to transport soldiers. Trade union membership was experiencing an explosive growth. Yet, tragically, in all the stormy events after Easter Week the labour movement played no independent role.

This outcome was by no means inevitable. The conditions for revolution were rapidly maturing. *What was lacking was a party and a leadership.* In the general election of 1918, the Labour Party stood down in favour of Republican candidates, and thus abdicated all claims to lead the movement. The leadership of the workers' organisations in the main accepted the slogan of the bourgeois nationalists: "Labour must wait." The idea that the working class must set aside its class interests and unite with the "liberal" bourgeoisie was not new then, yet it is still repeated today. The same old song was sung by the Mensheviks in Russia before 1917, as explained earlier. Lenin and Trotsky answered this nonsense a thousand times. In Ireland Connolly had demolished this argument on countless occasions. Even ealier Marx and Engels had explained many times the need for the workers to defend an independent class policy, even in the classical period of the bourgeois-democratic revolution.

This contradiction reflected itself in a bitter left-right split in the labour movement. There was, in effect, a civil war within the labour movement. The workers of Ireland clashed repeatedly against the limitations of bourgeois property and law. The Labour Party took no official stand on the Treaty, and was generally suspected of being in favour. But many were bitterly opposed. Liam Mellows' opposition to the Treaty led to his execution on December 8th, 1922. Mellows, who in effect succeeded Connolly, was a Marxist and organiser of the Fianna. Today not many people realise that the Fianna was founded by the socialist, Countess Markievicz, and started off as a socialist youth movement. Indeed until the 1970s that was still the case.

A hollow victory

Countess Markievicz denounced the Treaty to establish the Free State, and advocated James Connolly's ideal of a Workers' Republic. Those who supported the treaty were to be "set up to uphold English interests in Ireland, to block every ideal that the nation may wish to formulate, to block the teaching of Irish, to block the education of the poorest classes, to block, in fact, every bit of progress that every man and woman in Ireland today amongst working people desire to see put into force... A state run by the Irish people for the people before the rights of property. And I don't wish under the Soarstat (Free State) to anticipate that the directors of this and the capitalists' interests are to be at the head of it. My idea is the Workers' Republic for which Connolly died. And I say that that is one of the things that England wishes to prevent. She would sooner give us Home Rule than a democratic republic. It is the capitalists' interests that are pushing this treaty to block the march of the working people in England and Ireland..." (Quoted in Clifford King, op cit, pp. 113-4.)

Four days after the deal was announced, on 10th December 1921, a manifesto was issued (written from jail by Larkin) that stated: "We pledge ourselves now and in the future to destroy this plan of a nation's destruction. We propose carrying on the fight until we make the land of Erin a land fit for men and women - a Workers' Republic or Death." (Larkin, op cit., p. 236.)

For the working class, the proclamation of a "free Ireland" was a hollow victory. The crisis hit weak Irish capitalism hard. Unemployment was widespread and the wages of those in employment were low. Conditions were particularly bad in the rural areas. The conditions existed for an explosion of the class struggle. The Irish bourgeoisie, copying the tactics of their British class brothers, launched a policy of savage wage-cutting. In Waterford the farmers pushed through wage cuts of the agricultural labourers. The dock employers announced a cut in the already miserable wage of the men of two shillings a day. They were followed by the coal merchants and others.

The Irish employers went onto a general offensive, slashing wages and worsening conditions and hours. Police and troops were used to break strikes and end workers' occupations. The Cosgrave government intervened to force the workers to accept "mediation" resulting in wage cuts. The slogan "Labour must wait" now assumed its genuine content. *The workers and peasants were required by the bourgeoisie as foot soldiers in a war that was not their own. The men and women of no property were obliged to shed their blood for Ireland, but the fruits of victory were seized by the avaricious men of money.*

As late as 1922, the Labour Party won 17 seats in the Dail and actually polled more votes than the Anti-Treaty Panel. But it lacked a genuinely independent policy. Having thrown away the initiative, the workers' movement was forced onto the defensive. In the general election of August 1923, the Labour Party was reduced from 17 to 14 seats. Following a series of defeats, the trade unions went into steep decline. Membership fell from about 130,000 in 1923 to 95,000 in 1926. The Irish workers movement had been pushed back to where it stood before 1914. Despite everything, the working class remained loyal to Labour, which in 1927 won 22 seats and was the official opposition. But politically it was moving to the right, abandoning the ideas of Connolly.

The Labour Party, which had a big following in the early years of the Irish Free State and Republic, threw away its chance to become a decisive force. Its vote in Irish elections between 1923 and 1938 peaked at 12.6 percent in 1927 and fell to its lowest point in 1933, when it got a mere 5.7 percent. Overall, the Labour vote in this period oscillated around 9.7 percent. This could have provided a base from which to become a mass force, but in order to do this Labour would have had to put forward a radical policy, totally different from that of the two main bourgeois parties. In other words, it would have had to have gone back to the ideas and programme of Connolly. This the reformist leadership was not prepared to do, and that is what condemned the Party to impotence. At its tenth annual Conference in 1941, a resolution was passed by 51 votes to 16 that stated "This Conference is of the opinion that not enough is being done effectively to organise the Party throughout the country." The same song has been sung repeatedly ever since.

Partition

The betrayal of the nationalist bourgeoisie led to the division of the living body of Ireland. The Government of Ireland Bill introduced by Lloyd George in the autumn of 1920 became law on December 23rd. In effect, Ireland was partitioned. However, the Northern Ireland statelet was unviable from the beginning. This was virtually admitted by the fact that two counties with a Catholic majority - Fermanagh and Tyrone - had to be included in it in order to give it the slightest impression of viability. Had the inhabitants of these counties been asked their opinions in a referendum, they would certainly not have agreed to being separated from the South. But they were never asked. British imperialism deliberately detached the Six Counties in order to weaken Ireland and ensure its continued dominance.

The British imperialists were determined to hang onto the North for both economic and strategic reasons. Most of the industry of Ireland was concentrated in the North (textiles, shipbuilding). T.A. Jackson explains the economic motives for Partition:

"Ireland has ample natural resources. In 1923 she had ample labour for their development. But thanks to centuries of foreign exploitation she was starved of capital. Apart from the important commercial centre of Dublin there was massive investment only in the neighbourhood of Belfast, then the most populous city in the country. For Belfast, dominated by the linen and shipbuilding industries, the supreme need was diversification. This diversification could have arisen ideally from the impulse of developing the remainder of the country. There the great need was an adequate infrastructure, the development of electricity, turf, transport, building materials (especially lime and cement) and certain categories of engineering. The role of Belfast would have been the production of means of production for all Ireland.

"Partition destroyed all such prospects. Thus obviously state investment was essential and the state required access to the entire taxable capacity of the nation. But forty percent of this was held at the disposal of the English exchequer. How was the remaining sixty percent to finance recovery at a time when war and revolution had destroyed capital both in industry and agriculture, and delayed the replacement of more?" (T.A. Jackson, *Ireland her Own*, pp. 441-2.)

Even more decisive than the economic question was the strategic importance of Ireland's ports. As an island power, control of the seas was a vital question for British imperialism. They needed the ports of Ireland. That is why in the negotiations over the Free State, Lloyd George insisted stubbornly on the question of the Irish ports. As late as the Second World War, Churchill considered occupying Ireland, fearing that its ports might fall into German hands. This was spelt out by Winston Churchill in a letter to Andrews, the prime minister of Northern Ireland after the War:

"We were alone and had to face, single-handed, the fury of the German attack raining down death and destruction on our cities and, still more deadly, seeking to strangle our life by cutting off the entry to our ports of the ships which brought us food and the weapons we so sorely needed. Only one great channel remained open. That channel remained open because loyal Ulster gave us the full use of Northern Irish ports and waters and thus ensured the free workings of the Clyde and the Mersey. But for the loyalty of Northern Ireland and its devotion to what now became the cause of thirty governments of nations, we should have been confronted with slavery and death and the light, which now shines so strongly throughout the world, would have been quenched..." (Quoted in Clifford King, op cit, p. 20.)

The treaty guaranteed Britain access to certain harbour facilities, and in time of war, it would be given such further facilities as might be needed "for purposes of defence". The Six Counties would be given one month after the ratification of the treaty to opt out and remain part of the United Kingdom, in which case, a boundary commission was supposed to decide where the border would be.

Born in a bloody welter of sectarian pogroms, this "Ulster" was a reactionary sectarian creation from the beginning: "Roman Catholic families in the humble streets of Belfast were terrorized. Petrol was thrown into their houses and a hand grenade tossed in after it to start a blaze. People piled up their sticks of furniture and their children on to donkey carts and fled from their homes into the countryside where some, with nowhere to go, camped out in the open fields." (Clifford King, ibid, pp. 128.)

Before the First World War, Connolly and Larkin succeeded in uniting the working class in Belfast against the employers, cutting across the poison of sectarianism with class policies. In 1919 there were big strikes in Belfast, which shook the ruling class. In January 1919 the shipyard and engineering workers of Belfast went on strike and 20,000 workers marched on Belfast City Hall to demand a reduction in hours. The whole city was in a state of ferment. The strike soon became general: in addition to shipbuilding and engineering, gas, electricity, transport and most public services were out.

This coincided with a huge strike wave in Britain. In Belfast power was really in the hands of the strike committees and the Trades Council. In his book *Revolt on the Clyde*, the Scottish Communist Willie Gallagher - then a young shop steward from Glasgow - describes the feelings of trepidation he experienced when he went to Belfast to address a mass meeting of strikers. He need not have worried. The overwhelmingly Protestant working class of Belfast gave him an enthusiastic welcome. This posed a mortal threat to the ruling class both in Britain and Ireland, and it was this that determined their subsequent actions. Whatever their differences, the capitalists of England and Ireland, Catholic or Protestant, Green or Orange, were always ready to sink their differences and unite to defeat their own working class.

Fear of Revolution

A major element in the calculations of the British ruling class in forcing through Partition was fear of proletarian revolution in the north and south of Ireland. The first action of the Orange reaction was therefore to move to split the working class along religious lines. Without this, the victory of reaction and the partition of Ireland would have been impossible. The Orange Order through the press issued attacks against "Bolsheviks and Sinn Féiners" who were deceiving good Protestant workmen. When these attacks failed to break the strike, Carson himself gave a speech on the 12th July to a meeting of 120,000 Orangemen, in which he specifically singled out the labour movement for attack:

"They (Sinn Féin) have all kinds of insidious methods and organisations at work. Sometimes it is the Church. That does not make much way in Ulster. The more insidious method is tacking the Sinn Féin question and the Irish Republican question to the labour question....These men who come forward posing as the friends of labour care no more about labour than does the man in the moon. Their real object and the real insidious nature of their propaganda is that *it may mislead and bring about disunity among our own people*; and in the end, before we know where we are, we may find ourselves in the same bondage and slavery as in the rest of Ireland in the South and West." (Quoted in Clifford King, op cit, p. 96. our emphasis.)

This wily representative of the ruling class understood the central question very well: in order to keep the working class in subjugation it is necessary to bind them hand and foot to the chariot of the ruling class. It is necessary to convince them by all means that they have a community of interest with the class that oppresses and exploits them. It is precisely necessary to *mislead and bring about the disunity of the working class, by splitting it on religious, national and sectarian lines*. The division of Ireland was based from the beginning on the division of the working class. It will only be overcome when this division is done away with.

The workers of Belfast understood the meaning of this avalanche of sectarianism and through the labour organisations attempted to stop it, mobilizing 2,000 trade unionists to patrol the City and keep order. But as the strike waned, the initiative passed to the reactionaries. The police attacked pickets with great brutality. The poison of sectarianism was used most effectively by the bosses. The lumpen-proletarian rabble was mobilised by the Orange Order to whip up riots and pogroms. Catholic workers were thrown into the docks and pelted with rivets. There was looting and murder, shops and houses were smashed up by hooligans. The losers, as always, were the working class and the poorest sections of society. The plight of the Catholic workers in the Six Counties was dramatic:

"The unemployed amongst them found it difficult to get jobs, and others, who had jobs, were having to count themselves fortunate when they were able to hold onto them. The religious differences, always marked, being whipped up, as they were, had to produce in the opponents a bitterness and savagery, unusual even for Belfast, but surely not unanticipated by those currently responsible for the situation." (Clifford King, ibid, p. 127.)

In the pogroms, which lasted from June 1920 to June 1922, 1,766 people were injured and 428 killed. Nevertheless, the repression was not aimed exclusively at the Catholic community. Of the 9,000 workers sacked from their jobs after the defeat of the strike, one quarter were Protestants. The Protestant ascendancy was a cynical trick to divide the working class and ensure that the bosses would remain in control. However, in order to achieve this end, the oppression and discrimination of the Catholic population were built into the foundations of the "Ulster" six county statelet. Its first prime minister, Sir James Craig stated in 1932: "Ours is a Protestant government and I am an Orangeman." Two years later he emphasised the same point in the Stormont parliament: "I have always said that I am an Orangeman first and a politician and a member of this parliament afterwards... All I boast is that we have a Protestant parliament and a Protestant state." (P. Johnson, op. cit., p. 209.)

"Stick and Carrot"

Although Catholic workers have been and continue to have a higher chance of being unemployed than Protestant workers for much of the North's history, rates of Protestant unemployment have still been high. This gave the Orange Order both a "carrot and stick" to encourage Protestant workers to join. The Order was a place where workers could meet employers, and formally or informally receive job offers. On the other hand, particularly in rural areas, employers would be aware of who was a member and discriminate in job applications against those who were not.

As late as 1959, when the question was raised of allowing Catholics to join the Unionist Party or the Orange Order, Sir George Clark, the Grand Master of the Orange Order said that while Catholics might support Unionism through the ballot box, membership was another matter:

"I would draw your attention to the words 'civil and religious liberty'. The liberty, as we know, is the liberty of the Protestant religion. In view of this, it is difficult to see how a Roman Catholic, with the vast differences in our religious outlook, could be either acceptable within the Unionist Party as a member, or, for that matter, bring himself unconditionally to support its ideals. Further to this, an Orangeman is pledged to resist by all lawful means the ascendancy of the Church of Rome, abstaining from uncharitable words, actions and sentiments towards his Roman Catholic brethren." (P. Johnson, ibid, p. 210.)

Systematic discrimination against Catholics in jobs and housing continued in the Six Counties for decades, backed up by gerrymandering in elections that in practice denied them their civil rights. The Ulster Volunteers, a Protestant paramilitary force, were transformed in 1920 into a special constabulary to put down the Belfast riots, which they did with extreme violence. Later the RUC was backed up by the hated "Specials" - the A-Specials who were on duty all the time, the C-Specials who were for use in emergencies, and the notorious B-Specials, part-time policemen who played such a brutal role in suppressing the Civil Rights movement in 1968-9. In practice, all these bodies were open only to Protestants.

The repressive nature of the Six County statelet was underlined by the 1922

Civil Authorities (Special Powers) Act. It contained a catch-all offence that gave the authorities a free hand to deal with dissent:

"If any person does any act of such a nature as to be calculated to be prejudicial to the preservation of the peace or maintenance of order in Northern Ireland and not be specifically provided for in the regulations, he shall be deemed to be guilty of an offence against the regulations."

However, at key moments in the development of the class struggle the tendency for united action of Catholic and Protestant workers reasserted itself. In 1932, the Falls and Shankill rioted together against unemployment. Once again the Orange Order warned "loyal subjects of the King, the vital necessity of standing guard against communism". The class question was always uppermost in their minds. Sectarianism for the ruling class was only a means to an end.

Part Seven

The Russian revolution and Ireland

The Russian working class - as Trotsky had predicted in 1904 - came to power before the workers of Western Europe. The reader may wonder why several references and comparisons to the Russian revolution are included here. Whether one agrees or disagrees with Lenin, Trotsky and the Bolsheviks, whether one is an admirer of the October Revolution or an opponent, it is impossible to deny the impact that the Russian Revolution had on world history and on the development of the workers' movement internationally. Although there are many differences between Russia in 1917 and Ireland at the time (let alone today) there are also important parallels.

The "progressive" and "liberal" bourgeoisie had proved themselves incapable time and again of carrying out the tasks of the national democratic revolution. Like their counterparts in Russia the Irish bourgeois nationalists were tied to the imperialist powers by a thousand and one ties. In October 1917 in the place of the bourgeoisie who had proven themselves incapable of conducting a struggle against landlordism and imperialism, the Russian working class carried out the tasks of the bourgeois-democratic revolution, and immediately set about nationalising industry and passing over to the tasks of the socialist revolution. The bourgeoisie played an openly counterrevolutionary role, but was defeated by the workers in alliance with the poor peasants. The Bolsheviks then made a revolutionary appeal to the workers of the world to follow their example. Lenin knew very well that without the victory of the revolution in the advanced capitalist countries, especially Germany, the revolution could not survive isolated, especially in a backward country like Russia. What happened subsequently showed that this was absolutely correct. The setting up of the Third (Communist) International, the world party of socialist revolution, was the concrete manifestation of this perspective. The Russian Revolution is rich in lessons for the workers' movement everywhere. It had an effect in Ireland too.

Under the impact of the Russian Revolution, there was an attempt by William O'Brien and Cathal Shannon to revive the Socialist Party of James Connolly in February 1917. Unfortunately, after the death of Connolly the leadership demonstrated no real understanding of the tasks of the revolution and were hopelessly out of their depth. By 1921 most of the old leaders had left or had been expelled from the Socialist Party of Ireland (SPI). The SPI paper, *The Workers Republic*, reported: "At the weekly meeting, on 14th October, 1921, of the SPI the following resolution was passed:

"In accordance with our policy, and with our decision to adhere to the Communist International, we hereby take the preliminary steps to observe the second condition of affiliation to the Communist International and expel the following members:

"Cathal O'Shannon, William O'Brien, on the grounds of reformism, consecutive non-attendance at the Party, and consistent attempts to render futile all attempts to build up a Communist Party in Ireland."

The secretary of the newly-formed Communist Party of Ireland (CPI) was Roddy Connolly, James Connolly's son. Immediately the Communist Party of Ireland was faced in late 1921 with the national question in all its force. It took a principled position. When the terms of the Anglo-Irish Treaty became known, the Communist Party of Ireland opposed them and its position was set forth in a Manifesto.

The revolutionary traditions of 1916 were still fresh in the minds of the Irish working class. By contrast, the Nationalist Republicans argued that Labour must wait. To accommodate this, those who tried to revive the ideas of Connolly were expelled from the main Labour Party. The formation of an independent Communist Party in Ireland had the enthusiastic support of Lenin who correctly insisted on support to the Republican side during the Irish Civil war against the Free State. The Party did its duty in supporting the young Soviet Republic.

The Communist Party of Ireland stood for the establishment of a Workers' Republic. It led unemployed agitations and the seizing of the Rodunta building in Dublin. The Red flag was hoisted. However, in a matter of days the IRA police were used to clear the building and again made it safe for the private owner. The remarks of C.D. Greaves in his book *Liam Mellows and the Irish Revolution*, describe the situation at the time:

"On 14th December (1921) the Dáil assembled. In this predominantly petit-bourgeois gathering was concentrated the power of decision making of the whole nation. Outside, the Chambers of Commerce passed their resolutions. Country merchants, cattle dealers, manufacturers, great and small, took up from their natural superiors, agrarian and financial, the cry for order and for peace which alone could assure it.

"Also outside the labour movement. It gave no lead. Out of over a thousand branches and councils, only six even passed a resolution. *The Voice of Labour*, treated the issue as irrelevant. Only on the extreme left were warning voices heard. The Communist Party of Ireland described the treaty as a shameful betrayal. In fact, it was the first party in Ireland to condemn it:

"Larkin wired in similar terms from his American prison. These voices were lost in the general clamour. As the delegates took their seats both Republican police and Black and Tans were arresting the Wexford farm workers on strike for union recognition."

Dissention and splits

However, the CPI remained very small. It had maybe twenty or so active members. Moreover, it was riven with internal dissention and splits. The political level of the membership was low and they therefore looked to Moscow for a lead. This was what later undermined the party and reduced it to sterility.

In the early years of the Communist International, Lenin explained to the non-Russian Communist Parties the need to face to the masses and win them over from reformism. Most of the young and inexperienced Communists were tainted by ultra-leftism. They did not understand Lenin's position on the United Front, or his insistence on the need to penetrate the mass organisations.

The small Irish Communist Party failed either to penetrate the ranks of the Labour Party or the Republicans. Roddy Connolly advocated a turn to the Republican movement - which was a correct idea. But it was opposed by another faction that considered this tactic pointless and instead said the Party should devote its resources to direct action and political education. This doomed the CPI to sterility.

Finally, the Comintern dissolved the CPI at the insistence of Larkin, who refused to have anything to do with it. However, Larkin's attitude to the CPI seems to have been dictated by personal considerations. Larkin was elected to the International Executive of the Communist International in 1924 and this appears to have gone a bit to his head. Despite his undoubted personal courage and dedication to the movement, he was no theoretician and lacked Connolly's breadth of vision. In the end, he was only a class-conscious worker militant. As R.M. Fox noted:

"At no time in his life did Larkin advance any sharply defined view of the labour struggle. He was always a field worker not a staff man, and he accepted the vague socialist ideas of a future harmonious society which young men of that time could hear from many labour platforms. Sometimes he was inclined to speak with contempt of abstract theories as long-haired men and short-haired women who wanted to demonstrate their own cleverness instead of joining the fight to end intolerable evils." (R.M. Fox , op cit, p. 23.)

Surely Connolly would never have expressed himself in such terms. But contempt for theory was a hallmark of the tendency we know as Zinovievism, which acted as a stepping-stone along a path that led away from Leninism and towards Stalinism. The last thing that is required in a Stalinist party or international is people who can think for themselves.

The Communist International (CI) recognized Larkin's Irish Workers' League as its Irish section. Larkin led the party down a disastrous path. Against Lenin's explicit advice against splitting the trade unions, he set about building a "Red union" - the Workers' Union of Ireland (WUI) in an attempt to undermine and destroy the old ITWU. This shows that Larkin was more a syndicalist than a Communist. His dictatorial and capricious conduct inevitably led to a split. In 1926 a number of well-known CP leaders, including Roddy Connolly, set up the Workers' Party. However, after a promising start, the new party received a shattering blow when the Comintern refused to allow it to join and demanded that it disband.

At the Ninth Plenum of the Executive Committee of the CI, Larkin was directed to work in the existing mass trade unions in order to defeat the reformist leadership. But he was incapable of doing this. The Stalinist bureaucrats who were now in control in Moscow decided that he was useless for their purposes and demoted him. They concluded that the best way to build the Communist tendency in Ireland was to work in the Republican movement. For the wrong reasons they had come to a correct conclusion.

However, at this time the Russian Stalinists embarked upon an ultra-left binge, making a 180-degree turn. The policies of the so-called Third Period stated that all parties, except the Communist Parties, were objectively counter-revolutionary and "fascist". In Ireland that meant that the CP must denounce the Republicans and demand that their members leave the IRA and join the CP. The hysterical attacks of the CP alienated many rank and file Republicans. Instead of winning over the Republicans the tactics of the Stalinists only served to isolate the CP still further. This was at a time when a left wing was beginning to crystallise inside the Republican movement.

Left and Right Republicanism

It is a law that a mass petty bourgeois nationalist movement at a certain stage will tend to split on class lines. There has always been a left and right wing tendency in the Irish Republican movement, from its inception right down to the present day. The split of Sinn Féin in 1926 led to a separation between the openly bourgeois wing of De Valera (Fianna Fail) and the hard core of "physical force" Republicans, many of whom had left wing and socialist leanings, and were influenced by the tradition of Connolly and Mellows (socialist republicanism). There was a loose alliance of militant Republicans, left Socialists and Communists.

The IRA in practice had a more left wing policy than the Labour Party at this time. However, it threw away the possibilities by refusing to stand for election in the Dail. Independence on a capitalist basis had solved nothing for Ireland. Unemployment was a growing problem, made worse by the fact that in the years of the Great Depression after 1929, high unemployment in Britain made it impossible to find work through emigration across the Irish Sea. Under these circumstances, the IRA was recruiting at a fast rate and the circulation of *An Poblacht* (The Republic) was soaring.

All those on the Republican side gave their allegiance to the First Dail, which was elected by all the people of Ireland, whilst the Free State Dail represented less than half of the electorate of the South. This is the answer to those who believe that the people of Ireland voted for the Free State as opposed to a Republic. The Free State wanted to provoke a Civil War to crush the Republican movement. The Government therefore passed legislation for summary executions and other official reprisals.

These official reprisals included the killing of the IRA commanders for each of the four provinces of the north, Joe McKelvey, Rory O'Connor, Dick Barret and Liam Mellows. James Connolly was Liam Mellows' mentor, and this brave republican saw national liberation in terms of economic as well as political terms. Indeed, it was important for the bourgeoisie of the Free State to eliminate all those who had a Marxist awareness.

Peadar O'Donnell, who advocated a socialist society, attempted to set up soviets in the area under his command area in Donegal. The landlords were evicted and the land handed over to the peasants and the employers forced to become workers in their own factories. Naturally, Peadar, was on the reprisals list. He was known and respected not only in Ireland, but also by the socialist community worldwide.

In the late 1920s and early 1930s a left wing emerged in the IRA led by O'Donnell, Frank Ryan, George Gimore and Michael Price, who tried to defend Connolly's idea of a Workers' Republic. In the class battles of the 1930s, the left wing of the Republican movement tried to represent the interests of the working class, the unemployed and the poor farmers. In the 1930s there was a Communist wing in the IRA. The left-right split in the Republican movement was illustrated with brutal clarity in the Spanish Civil War when Eoin O'Duffy, formerly the IRA's liason officer for the Six Counties, organised the pro-fascist blue shirts who fought on the side of General Franco in Spain.

A Republican Congress preparatory Conference held in Athlone in April 1931, issued a Manifesto which proclaimed:

"We believe that a Republic of a united Ireland will never be achieved except through a struggle which uproots Capitalism on its way. 'We cannot conceive of a free Ireland with a subject working class: We cannot conceive of a subject Ireland with a free working class.' This teaching of Connolly represents the deepest instincts of the oppressed Irish nation." (Quoted by W.K. Anderson, op cit, p. 134.)

The Athlone Manifesto urged that "A Congress of Republican opinion must be assembled to make the Republic a main issue dominating the whole political field and to outline what are the forms of activity that move to its support."

The IRA set up a left-wing party under the name of Saor Eire and at its first congress in 1931 it described itself as "an Organisation of Workers and Working Farmers" with socialist goals. In October 1931 Saor Eire was denounced by the Catholic Bishops of Ireland as "frankly communistic in its aims". The Bishops went on to say that Saor Eire and the IRA, "whether separate or in alliance", were "sinful and irreligious" and that "no Catholic can lawfully be a member of them." (Quoted by W.K. Anderson, ibid, p. 133.) One day later the IRA, Saor Eire and ten other radical Republican organisations were declared illegal under a Constitution (Declaration of Unlawful Associations) Order.

All the conditions were maturing for an upsurge of the class struggle in Ireland, but the class divisions in Irish society were obscured and complicated by the national question. The IRA's nationalism prevented it from developing a worked out revolutionary programme and policy. At the first Republican Congress, in September 1934, Roddy Connolly, with the backing of his sister Nora and other delegates, proposed that "this Congress definitely declare that an Irish Workers' Republic be its slogan of action." The United Front resolution was passed by 99 votes to 84. But there was a major split over the direction of the Republican movement. It has persisted ever since. At bottom it is a split along class lines.

Republicanism and Stalinism

There was every possibility of winning over the revolutionary elements in the Republican movement to Communism. The IRA was originally born out of a combination of the ICA on the one hand and the Irish Volunteers on the other. Thus, a class cleavage was present in its ranks from the very beginning. The Marxist element (republican socialism) always remained as a strand. That is why in some areas during the war of independence, the IRA took the land from the big landowners and in other areas formed soviets of agricultural workers. In other words, the Republican movement divided on class lines between the supporters of the working class on the one hand, and the bourgeoisie and private property on the other. The latter element within the IRA took the side of the employers and the landowners.

The contradiction already surfaced in 1923. Many members of the IRA supported Roddy Connolly, and others O'Brien, and still others opposed socialism altogether. Moreover the problems of 1923 were related to the international perspective. The most revolutionary elements naturally sympathized with the Russian Revolution. James Larkin was elected to the Executive Committee of the Communist International at the Fifth congress in 1924, the year Lenin died. Having a good instinct for tactics, he intervened in the tenth session to support the proposal of the British Party to attempt to form a united front with the Labour Party (a position that Lenin had advocated). But before long the weak Irish Communist Party succumbed to Stalinism, with fatal results.

Had the Communist International remained firm on the positions of Lenin and Trotsky, the victory of the world revolution would have been ensured. Unfortunately, the Comintern's formative years coincided with the Stalinist counter-revolution in Russia, which had a disastrous effect on the Communist Parties of the entire world. The Stalinist bureaucracy, having acquired control in the Soviet Union developed a very conservative outlook. The theory that socialism can be built in one country - an abomination from the standpoint of Marx and Lenin - really reflected the mentality of the bureaucracy which had had enough of the storm and stress of revolution and sought to get on with the task of "building socialism in Russia". That is to say, they wanted to protect and expand their privileges and not "waste" the resources of the country in pursuing world revolution. On the other hand they feared that revolution in other countries could develop on healthy lines and pose a threat to their own domination in Russia, and therefore, at a certain stage, sought actively to prevent revolution elsewhere.

Theory of "two stages"

Instead of pursuing a revolutionary policy based on class independence, as Lenin had always advocated, they proposed an alliance of the Communist Parties with the "national progressive bourgeoisie" (and if there was not one easily at hand, they were quite prepared to invent it) to carry through the democratic revolution, and afterwards, later on, in the far distant future, when the country had developed a fully fledged capitalist economy, fight for socialism. This policy represented a complete break with Leninism and a return to the old discredited position of Menshevism - the theory of the "two stages".

Larkin, unlike Connolly, was no theoretician. He lacked a deep grounding in the ideas and methods of Marxism. In the struggle between Stalin and the Left Opposition he was out of his depth. When asked by Bukharin if he would like to speak in the debate, he declined, saying that "the issue was one between the men and women of Russia, and that it would be an impertinence (!) on his part to speak." (Larkin, op. cit., p. 262.)

Despite his sterling features, Larkin was not fitted to build a serious Communist Party in Ireland. Although the Irish Communists were heroic people who fought against the fascist Blueshirts both in Ireland and in Spain, under the baleful influence of Stalinism, the Party was unable to penetrate the masses and remained a sect. Milotte notes that the "Communist Party's twists and turns in the 1937-9 period had a devastating effect on party organisation - which virtually disintegrated", and he adds that "Party activities now consisted almost entirely of discussing what others were doing." (Larkin, ibid., p. 135.)

Later on, when the CP collapsed into the Officials, they combined reformist opportunism with some correct ideas. In the main their criticism of the armed struggle was from a pacifist and opportunist standpoint. At least partly as a result some of the most militant youth were repelled and moved over to the breakaway Provisional IRA, with disastrous consequences.

A pernicious role has been played by reformism and Stalinism in Ireland. But now, with the collapse of the USSR, Stalinism is in decline everywhere. The best elements who previously looked to Moscow or Beijing are rethinking their positions and looking for a genuine revolutionary tendency.

Part Eight

The Thirties

The Thirties were a period of class struggle nationally and internationally. The Wall Street Crash of 1929 was followed by the Great Depression. There was mass unemployment everywhere. It affected the working class across the whole of Ireland and Britain. Everywhere the class struggle was on the increase. This was reflected in a left tendency within the Republican movement, where, as we have seen, the socialist tradition left behind by Connolly had never disappeared.

In Britain the betrayal of Ramsay MacDonald led to the fall of the Labour government and the establishment of the National Government in which the Tories dominated. The ruling class launched a savage campaign of cuts, slashing the already miserable benefits of the unemployed. This led to mass demonstrations of the unemployed in Britain (the Hunger Marches) and the Invergordon mutiny in Scotland, when the sailors struck against a reduction in their wage.

In the same year as the Invergordon mutiny there was a ferment among the masses in the Six Counties. The conditions of the working class in Belfast were appalling. 37 percent of houses were either overcrowded or just unfit for habitation. The situation in other parts was even worse: 50 percent of houses in Fermanagh were unfit to live in. Unemployment, which stood at 100,000 just before the War, was proportionately higher than in Britain. It is true that the Catholics were in a worse position because they suffered from discrimination and police brutality, but there was extreme poverty and deprivation in working class Protestant areas like the Shankill.

There was a campaign of agitation against the cut in welfare benefits imposed by the government. This was a wonderful episode in the workers' struggle for better conditions. There was a fight against the Poor Law Guardians of Belfast, who were controlled by the Unionist Party. The Guardians had imposed extremely harsh conditions on unemployed workers. A march up the Newtownards Road was organised by the Revolutionary Workers Group. The demonstrators were attacked by the sectarian bigots with the aid of the police. The demonstrators were unemployed Catholics and Protestants, marching together. *This showed the possibility for united class action, once a fighting lead is given.*

Thousands of Outdoor Relief workers took to the streets to protest against the government's measures. Some of these protests ended up in clashes with the police and in a series of riots, with a large number of people being arrested. The worst riot occurred on the Falls Road where two protesters, Samuel Baxter and John Keenan, were shot dead.

The Outdoor Relief workers replied with a massive protest to Queens Square, organised by the Revolutionary Workers Groups. There were about 40,000 workers in Queens Square on the night of 11th October 1932. They came from all parts of Belfast, and from Derry and Coleraine. Four hundred workers set out to walk from Dublin to Belfast, but as they reached the border the RUC stopped them and turned most of them back. But some did manage to reach Belfast and took part in the march.

These stormy events give the lie to those who claim that the Protestant people of the Six Counties form one reactionary mass, and that it is impossible for workers of both communities to unite in struggle against the bosses. On the contrary, at every decisive moment of the class struggle there has been a clear tendency towards class unity which alone can cut across sectarianism. Connolly and Larkin always based themselves on this. If the workers are given a clear lead they will always respond. The problem is when such a lead is not given, or when an incorrect lead is given. It is necessary to draw all the conclusions from this fact.

Bourgeoisie fails

From the beginning, the Six County statelet was not economically viable and had to be maintained by huge subsidies from London. However, the situation in the South was even worse. Only in the recent period has there been a significant upturn in the Southern economy. For decades the situation was so bad that many Irish people emigrated to England and to the North in search of jobs. In 1947 Stormont felt obliged to pass a Safeguarding Employment Act to limit rising emigration from the Republic.

The Six Counties' economic dependence on Britain was such that in the mid-Sixties one authority, R.J. Lawrence, calculated that "if Ulster were independent and had to pay for her own defence and for diplomatic consular and other 'imperial' services, she would have either to cut domestic spending by some £50 million a year or raise that sum by taxation. Either course would be catastrophic." (Quoted by P. Johnson, op. cit., p. 216.)

Decades after achieving formal independence, the South remained heavily dependent upon British capitalism. The post boxes were painted green, but English pounds remained legal tender both north and south of the border. Until very recently, the South remained a predominantly agrarian, economically backward country. Between 1945 and 1961 the population of the South of Ireland declined still further. It lost 500,000 people. This figure alone shows that the Southern bourgeoisie has not succeeded in developing Ireland or even achieving genuine independence. An official report on economic development noted in 1958:

"After 35 years of native government people are asking whether we can achieve an acceptable degree of economic progress. The common talk among parents in the towns, as well as in rural Ireland, is of their children having to emigrate as soon as their education is completed in order to secure a reasonable standard of living." (P. Johnson, ibid., pp. 216-7.)

The achievement of formal independence for the South on a capitalist basis solved nothing for the people of Ireland. Until recently, economic emigration sapped the population of the South. The Southern capitalists are utterly dependent on foreign capital - British, American, and European. The Irish language has declined dramatically. The number of native Irish speakers had fallen to under 70,000 by 1966 - that is, less than 20 percent of the level at the time of independence. Since then the situation has deteriorated still further. Connolly's warnings about what would happen in an independent capitalist Ireland have been cruelly confirmed.

Moves towards reunification

During this period the IRA was engaged in its border campaign (1956-62), which was doomed to failure. It is sufficient to note that the IRA was compelled to operate from bases in the South. *They had no real base in the North.* By 1962, they had to admit that the whole episode had ended in failure. *The New York Times* wrote: "They have been condemned by the most deadly of all judgments, political indifference (…) The present generation know that if Partition is ever to be ended it must be by peaceful arrangements. " (*The New York Times*, 26th February, 1962.)

The economy of the South improved somewhat in the course of the 1960s, and emigration was virtually halted. In an attempt to maintain the differential with the South, the government of the Six Counties launched its own plan for economic development, calling for the creation of 65,000 new jobs. Over a seven-year period (1963-9), nearly sixty new factories were established in the North, where the level of unemployment went down from four times to three times the United Kingdom average.

The relations between London and Dublin at this time were excellent. Why should they not be, when the Republic was little more than a satellite of British imperialism? *In fact, there was a movement towards the integration of the North and South by common agreement of the Irish and British ruling classes.* Sean Lemass entered into negotiations with Terence O'Neill (1963-69) to bring about closer relations with the Six Counties, with the encouragement of London. In 1965 O' Neill and Lemass exchanged visits. It was at this time that Lemass famously claimed Connolly's ideas to be outdated…

The fact that British imperialism was preparing the way for a handover of the North is not seriously in doubt. London was prodding O'Neill to enter into closer relations with the South and to introduce reforms to head off a social explosion. In November 1968, after a cabinet meeting, O'Neill announced a five-point reform programme, including a new system to allocate housing, the abolition of the business vote in local elections and a review of the Special Powers Act. One week later the Electoral Law (Amendment) Act was passed, abolishing university seats and multiple votes in parliamentary elections and providing for a new electoral boundary commission.

On 9th December he made a television broadcast, beginning with the words: "Ulster stands at the crossroads", asking for the collaboration of both Protestants and Catholics and warning Unionists that both Harold Wilson and Edward Heath had told him that any attempt to sabotage the reform programme could lead to direct intervention by Westminster. At this stage, probably the majority of Catholics in the Six Counties would have been prepared to settle for these reforms. After his retirement O'Neill claimed: "I had won the trust of Catholics as no previous prime minister had ever been able to do. But I was unable to restore to them the rights that small-minded men had removed from them during the first years of Northern Ireland's existence." (Quoted in P. Johnson, ibid, p. 223.)

However, the carefully laid plans for reform were immediately shattered against the rock of sectarianism. For generations British imperialism had created this Frankenstein's monster. At a critical point it was unable to control the monster created by its own hands. The reforms from the top encouraged the rapid rise of the Civil Rights movement in the Six Counties, which was met by a ferocious backlash on the part of the Loyalist bigots and Unionist reactionaries. The moves towards closer links caused a crisis among the Unionists. In 1966 and again in 1967, there were attempts to oust O'Neill from the leadership of the Unionist Party. His action in inviting Lemass to Belfast caused a furore of opposition within Unionism, and helped to spark off the events of 1968.

The Civil Rights movement

The Civil Rights movement was really a reflection of the international situation and especially the revolutionary movement in France in May 1968. This was entirely in line with Irish history. The revolt of the United Irishmen was inspired by the French revolution of 1789-93. The Easter Rising of 1916 was a direct result of the imperialist World War. The students of the north of Ireland were no different to their counterparts in Paris. The Civil Rights movement began with a march of 2,500 demonstrators from Coalisland to Dungannon on Saturday, 24 August, 1968. Protestant bigots staged vicious attacks against the demonstrators. When the marchers attempted to cross Craigavon bridge, the police made a baton charge. Riot equipment was used, stones thrown and 88 people were injured - 77 civilians and 11 police.

It is important to note that the IRA had little or nothing to do with the Civil Rights movement, which was influenced by Marxism and revolutionary ideas. The movement contained both Catholics and Protestants. In particular the Derry Young Socialists played a key role, fighting the bigots on the barricades. On 19th April there was a ferocious battle in Derry in which the people fought back against their tormentors. The figures tell their own story. This time 209 police were injured, against 79 civilians. Faced with a barrage of petrol bombs, the authorities were forced to use armoured cars. The next day, O'Neill resigned and the whole reform programme was consigned to the dustbin.

The only way to win reforms is through mass struggle. In general, meaningful reforms are the by-product of revolution. Matters from now on would be decided, not in the corridors of Stormont and Westminster, but on the streets, where a bloody struggle for power was unfolding. On 18th March, the Civil Rights Association announced that it would continue and intensify its campaign of civil disobedience. It put forward a programme of transitional demands, including: One person, one vote in local government elections; votes at eighteen; an independent Boundaries Commission to determine electoral boundaries; a fair housing allocation system; anti-discrimination laws for employment; a review of the Special powers Act and disbandment of the B-Specials.

Bernadette Devlin won an election in mid-Ulster at this time and correctly went to Westminster to put her case, which she did very effectively.

The Provisional IRA

The so-called "traditional Republicans" and the socialist Republicans have long formed two clearly identifiable and contradictory tendencies. In the Thirties and Forties we had the traditionalist Sean Russell and the Republican Socialist Frank Ryan. Sean Cronin and Ruairi O'Bradaigh represented the self-same class tendencies in the fifties. Although at the time it was not so clear, these leaders represented two different tendencies - and, in the last analysis, *two antagonistic class interests.*

The socialist trend in Republicanism was itself divided between two contradictory tendencies - *the Stalinist reformists and the revolutionary Socialists.* In the sixties Cathal Goulding represented the left wing and Ruairi O'Bradaigh the "traditionalists". In the Sixties most of the traditionalists left the movement. But they remained a major influence. After the failure of the 1950s border campaign, the IRA fell under the control of the Stalinists, who steered it away from the old militarism - which was very good - and towards reformism and pacifism - which was very bad.

When the Republicans left the prisons in the sixties, we find a heavy influence of the CPNI (that became the CPI). Roy Johnson of the British Communist Party was seconded to the leadership of the Republican Movement. By this time the left wing had control of the leadership. This was a golden opportunity to return it to the revolutionary class traditions of Connolly, but unfortunately the Stalinists took the movement down the reformist road, with disastrous consequences.

1966 was a turning point. A number of young people began to join the movement. They were radical in outlook and looking for the revolutionary road. However this did not fit in with the schemes of the then leadership of the Republican Movement. The latter did not have a revolutionary perspective and consequently were taken by surprise by the events of 1969, when the North was moving fast in the direction of civil war. On 12th August in the Catholic Bogside district of Derry the barricades went up in response to attacks by the combined forces of the RUC and Protestant mobs. Having fought off the forces of reaction, the revolutionary youth raised Republican flags and proclaimed the Bogside Free Derry.

The Stalinist leadership was taken aback by the revolutionary movement in the North, for which they were completely unprepared. They had moved away from the armed struggle, but had made the mistake of getting rid of their weapons. Here, however, the question of arms was posed point-blank, in the first place to defend the Catholic workers' districts. The young people inevitably looked to the IRA to provide arms and defend the Catholic areas against pogroms. But no arms were forthcoming. The revolutionary youth wrote on the walls the ironical slogan: IRA = "I ran away". The revolutionary potential was clearly present, but the revolution was not armed. What was needed was an armed workers defence force, based on the trade unions, on the lines of Connolly's ICA.

Nature abhors a vacuum. When there was no revolutionary force ready and able to take over the leadership, the forces of reaction raised their head. Fearing the development of a revolutionary movement in the North, the Irish bourgeoisie took steps to divert it along nationalist lines. As a key part of this strategy they deliberately split the IRA, which was too left wing for their liking. Large amounts of money were supplied to the right wing, conservative, militaristic elements to set up a rival organisation, the Provisional IRA, in opposition to the "Officials", as they became known.

The split in the Republican movement did not take place in a straightforward manner. Before the Provisionals were formed in January 1970 there were a number of minor splits. In the 3 months prior to the formation of the Provisionals in January 1970. Many of those who had left the IRA in 1966, because of the introduction of Marxist policies, returned to join the Provisonals. These were fanatical anti-Communists. This development suited the interests of the ruling class in the South very well, and they supported it by all the means at their disposal.

It was the Southern state intelligence services that set up and organised the Provisionals. The money and the guns of the Provos were supplied through the agency of two right-wing ministers in the Dublin government - Blaney and Houghey. Large sums came from the USA, and were directed to the anti-Communist, pro-sectarian elements in the winter of 1968-69. Paradoxically, the leading element was an Englishman living in the Republic under the name of Sean MacStiofain.

When the population of the Six-Counties defiantly resisted the Stormont repression and fought the local forces of "law and order" to a standstill, the Stormont government had to call in the British Army to suppress the insurgents. But they were not the only ones who wanted such an intervention. *The truth is that both the British and Irish ruling classes were terrified of the prospect of social revolution in the Six Counties that could easily spread to the South and to Britain. They conspired together to crush the revolution at all costs.*

Derry Young Socialists

In Derry, thanks in no small measure to the Marxist leadership of the Young Socialists, the Bogside district was under the control of the Derry Citizens Defence Committee. Following a stone-throwing incident, the RUC began to attack. There was an imminent danger of a pogrom. As a result, the people of the Bogside and Creggan rose up to defend their areas, setting up barricades. Despite fierce fighting, the forces of the state were unable to penetrate their defences and enter the Bogside. Jack Lynch, the Fianna Fail prime minister in Dublin, made a broadcast in which he informed the people of Ireland that he was asking Britain to apply for a United Nations peacekeeping force, since Stormont was "no longer in control". *This was a direct instigation to Britain to intervene in the North to re-establish order.*

The British government promptly took its cue from Dublin. On 14th August British troops were ordered into Derry by Labour Prime Minister James Callaghan. The next day they entered Belfast. By the end of that week there were 6,000 British troops in the Six Counties. The excuse - accepted by many, including it must be stated the Lefts in the British Labour Party and organisations like the SWP, who subsequently became uncritical cheerleaders for the Provos - was that they had come to defend the Catholics and keep the peace. But nothing was solved. In the five years of the O'Neill government only three people had died in sectarian incidents. In the summer of 1969 nine people were killed, 150 were wounded by gunfire, 500 houses were destroyed and over 2,000 people were made homeless. And that was nothing compared to the horrors that lay ahead.

At first the British troops had been welcomed by many Catholics. But soon the real nature of the forces of British imperialism became clear. Their main purpose was to destroy the revolutionary movement that was developing in the North. *Their main target was the "Communists", as they made clear.* This aim was shared by the bourgeois rulers in the South, who used the Provisional IRA for this purpose. Nowadays it has been forgotten or is not known by many, but the Provos were viciously anti-Communist. Their activities included the burning of Marxist books. In the words of Connor Cruise O'Brien, "There was no 'taint of Communism' about them, nothing puzzling or foreign at all (...) These Provisionals weren't like the old crowd - they were getting the guns and they were ready to use them." (Connor Cruise O'Brien, *States of Ireland*, London, 1972.)

Some IRA people fought against the British and the RUC, although the Provisionals have always denied this, because these were the people who later joined the Republican socialist movement. But the Provos had most of the arms, and that resulted in their rapid growth at the expense of the left wing. When the repressive face of British imperialism was revealed, the revolutionary youth lined up to join the only people who offered them what they were demanding. The Provos grew by leaps and bounds, leaving the Officials standing. Before 1968 the IRA had no real base in the Six Counties. They played at best a secondary role in the mass Civil Rights movement. But virtually overnight they got a mass base. They moved into the Catholic areas of Belfast and Derry, setting up bases, arms caches and safe houses.

No-go areas were set up in many areas of Belfast and Derry. Citizen Defence Committees were set up to police these areas. These committees were in fact controlled by the Official IRA. More correctly, the elements who organised the no-go areas were the rank and file of the Official IRA, who later formed, the IRSP. There were deep contradictions within the Officials. In 1970 there was an emergency Ard Fheis, as a result of what had happened in August 1969. After the Provisionals were formed what was left behind was a mixed bag, and it soon emerged that there were serious differences in the ranks.

The leadership of the Officials did not oppose the negotiations which took place with the British Civil Service. The truth is that both the Official IRA and the Provisional leaderships took part in these negotiations. The conditions were that control of the no-go areas should be taken out of the hands of the rank and file, and handed back to the Republican leadership. *The British informed the Officials that the rank and file were "Communists" and that these no-go areas were being referred to as Soviets.*

Even though many in the leadership of the Officials did not mind the term Communist, this was a period of much anti-communist propaganda being thrown at them by the Provisionals. While posing as the defenders of the Catholic areas, however, the Provos were pursuing their own agenda. *The real aim of the Provos was to cut across the Civil Rights movement and undermine the "Communist" Officials, pushing the border issue once more to the forefront.* They sought to sever the link between the national and social aspects of the struggle in order to promote the former and relegate the latter to some distant future. The Provos had the great advantage of possessing the arms that the young people so desperately needed. They offered guns and what seemed to be a simple policy: "Get the British troops out".

In fact, the policy of the Provos was a delusion. To imagine that it was possible to defeat the might of the British Army in single combat was madness, as subsequently became only too clear. Nevertheless, that was their aim at the time. The greatest tragedy in recent Irish history is that many of the most heroic and self-sacrificing youth were seduced by the siren call of the Provisional IRA. It has taken thirty years and 3,500 deaths for it to become clear that the whole strategy, tactics and methodology of the Provisionals was fatally flawed.

The immediate effect of the methods of the Provos was to exacerbate sectarianism. Yet the only hope for defeating reaction was to cut across the sectarian divide. This was possible, on condition that the correct policies and tactics had been pursued. Without any leadership there were many local initiatives to combat sectarianism. In August 1969 a meeting of 9,000 workers at the big Harland and Wolff shipyard declared their opposition to the sectarian intimidation of Catholics. Joint patrols of Catholic and Protestant workers were established in the Ardoyne and several other areas.

By the summer of 1969 local defence groups - almost all of them non-sectarian - had been formed in Ballymurphy, Springhill, Turf Lodge, New Barnsley, Springmartin, Highfield and Clonard. If this tendency had been encouraged, and the patrols had been armed, an entirely different perspective would have opened up. Instead, the sectarian paramilitary organisations of both sides launched a vicious campaign of intimidation to drive people of the other religion from their homes and create separate enclaves. Families were burned out of their houses just on the basis of their supposed religious affiliation. This systematic criminal activity was intended to reinforce the sectarian divide and turn it into an abyss. It succeeded only too well.

Part Nine

Bloody Sunday

At first, the British government, which for a long time had no direct involvement in Six-County rule, attempted a civil rights reform, but with significant concessions to Unionism, such as the replacement of the B-Specials by the UDR. But the imperialists quickly saw that the undemocratic and repressive government and social discrimination would make a pacification of the Province impossible. These were necessary features of Six-County government because it was the last corner of colonial rule in Ireland, and colonial rule always requires coercive government. They attempted to introduce reforms. But this was soon cut across by events.

On 6th February 1971 a British soldier was killed. To this day it is not clear who was responsible, although at the time it was attributed to the Provos. In August, William Faulkner announced the introduction of internment without trial. The war had begun in earnest. The death toll grew remorselessly: from only 25 in 1970 to 173 in 1971. On 30th January 1972, British paratroops shot dead 13 unarmed demonstrators in Derry. A fourteenth innocent victim died later. This was a major turning point. The British army showed on Bloody Sunday in Derry its determination to shoot peaceful civil rights demonstrators off the streets. Pacifism was no answer to this. The immediate reaction of the masses opened up the possibility of developing a broad movement against repression and imperialism. But there was nobody to give the necessary leadership.

Bloody Sunday caused a wave of anger and revulsion. The next Sunday 70,000 people marched in Newry. On the day of the funerals, 60,000 people marched in Dublin, which was shut down by a general strike. A three-day general strike was called in the North, sweeping through Derry, Newry, Strabane and other towns. A significant number of Protestant workers joined the strike, especially in Derry (Dupont, Post Office engineers and others). In Belfast, Queen's University was closed by strike action on the part of both students and staff, as was Magee College in Derry and Coleraine University, where 400 people heard Ted Grant debate with a Unionist MP on the subject of "the Workers' Republic."

The pacifistic civil rights leaders were shell-shocked and more or less threw in the towel. Later the British imperialists unleashed the loyalist terror campaign against random Catholics. These events unfortunately acted as a very effective recruiting sergeant for the Provos, who grew very rapidly at the expense of everyone else. The youth was eager for revenge, and the Provos had the guns. The Six Counties entered into a vicious downward spiral of tit-for-tat sectarian killings and bombings. On one day alone, "Bloody Friday", 22 Provisional IRA bombs killed eleven people.

The strategy of the Provisionals appeared to many to be the only alternative. They promised instant and easy solutions based on the gun and the bomb. But this so-called "practical" solution was based on a false assumption - that the British imperialists would get tired of all the mayhem and leave. Thirty years later we are still waiting. Events have clearly demonstrated that it is impossible to bomb the Six Counties into a United Ireland and force the British to leave. All that the Provos succeeded in doing was to push Protestants into the arms of Orange reaction and British imperialism, split the working class right down the middle and strengthen the forces of the British state. They have achieved precisely the opposite of what was intended.

The Sunningdale Agreement

The Northern Ireland Act, which became law on 21st November 1973, abolished the 1920 Act and replaced Stormont with a new Assembly. The Sunningdale agreement of December 1974, signed by Liam Cosgrave, accepted that no changes could take place in Northern Ireland without the agreement of a majority of its people. On the other hand, the Ulster Unionists accepted the idea of a "Council of Ireland", formed from the Dail and the new Assembly. The Irish bourgeoisie had not the slightest interest in a united Ireland. They would not relish the prospect of paying out the huge sums paid annually to Belfast by the British Exchequer. Nor would they particularly like the idea of a large population of resentful and disaffected Protestants in a United Ireland.

The Provisionals have been negotiating with the British on and off since 1972. On 1st January 1974 Britain's first Secretary of State for Northern Ireland, William Whitelaw, brought together representatives from the moderate Unionist parties, the Alliance Party and the Social Democratic and Labour Party into a power sharing executive. In addition, Whitelaw established a "Council of Ireland," which would provide the Dublin government with a consultative, though powerless, role in matters of concern to both parts of Ireland. *In essence, this is the same as the Good Friday Agreement.* But it immediately broke down.

The Loyalists were outraged at the prospect of sharing power with "disloyal" representatives of the nationalist community, as well as at the idea of Dublin having even a consultative role in the affairs of the North. The anti-power sharing Loyalists nevertheless joined the coalition as the United Ulster Unionist Council (UUUC), won 11 out of 12 seats in the general election held in February 1974. The UUUC electoral victory was not sufficient to bring down the power-sharing executive, so they carried the struggle onto the streets, organizing a strike to paralyse the Province and sabotage the agreement. They demanded "a Protestant parliament for a Protestant people."

The Ulster Workers' Council strike began in May 1974. The industrial action of the UWC was backed by intimidation and violence from the UDA, UVF, and other Loyalist paramilitaries allied under an umbrella organisation, the Ulster Army Council. By these methods they succeeded in shutting down much of the Six Counties' economic activity. The real strength of the UWC strike was their control of the electricity-generating industry. With virtually the entire blue-collar workforce on strike, and the remaining white-collar staff either intimidated by Loyalist paramilitaries, or in sympathy with the strike, power cuts became longer and longer until the Unionist members of the power sharing executive resigned and the executive collapsed on 28th May.

The UWC strike had a purely reactionary and sectarian character. Nevertheless, it also showed the colossal power of the working class, and its ability to bring the system to its knees through collective effort. In the future the workers of the Six Counties will find a more productive use for this power, once they are led by men and women who represent their true class interests.

The collapse of the Assembly ushered in a very bloody period in Irish history. London saw no alternative but to impose direct rule. The forces of sectarianism were unleashed, with a big increase in violence on the part of the Loyalist paramilitaries in the North. During the UWC strike, car bombs attributed to Loyalist paramilitaries were exploded in Dublin and Monaghan in the South of Ireland, killing 27 people (though recently revealed documents have suggested that the MI6 British intelligence forces may have actually been responsible for the bombings).

The Ulster Defense Regiment was formed in 1970 as a "home guard" branch of the British Army. Very soon after its formation, it became known that many members of the UDR used their connections with the British Army, and their access to weapons and ammunition, as well as intelligence files, to participate in sectarian murders of Irish Catholics in the occupied Six Counties. Many members of the UDR were also members of Loyalist death squads, such as the Ulster Volunteer Force or the Ulster Freedom Fighters. In a period of nine months

(January to September 1975) 196 civilians were murdered in sectarian violence, in addition to many republican deaths.

In March 1975 a feud erupted between the UDA and the UVF. The feud was short-lived and resulted in few deaths. Later that same year, the UVF was legally banned, after a UVF bombing claimed 11 lives in October. Relations between the RUC and the Loyalists began to deteriorate, resulting in Loyalist communities with strong ties to the paramilitaries beginning the practice of policing their own neighbourhoods rather than relying on the RUC. Thereafter a bloody stalemate persisted, punctuated by sporadic outbreaks of new feuds amongst the loyalist gangs.

Seamus Costello

There were many Republicans who would have "no truck with socialism"; others blinded by military failure and personal disillusionment were shortly to turn their backs on the national question and to reject militancy in any shape or form. The former was to form the Provos and the latter became the Workers Party. But there were those who were moving in the direction of revolutionary Marxism, among whom a place of honour must be reserved for Seamus Costello.

A committed Republican from the age of 15, Seamus Costello was a veteran in the ranks of the IRA and Sinn Féin from the early fifties. He participated enthusiastically in the military campaign against the British occupation of the northern Six Counties in the 1950s. But he was soon to realise that heroism and self-sacrifice were not enough. The campaign fought in the mountainous border regions did not have the desired result. On the other hand, people throughout Ireland were more concerned with the pressing social problems of the day, with increasing unemployment and mounting emigration. He advocated a more political approach and closer links with the workers' movement.

Between 1963 and 1967 the republican movement underwent a radical change in outlook, policies and activities. Seamus Costello was one of those most directly responsible for that change. Seamus continued to accept that the fight against the British was correct and necessary, but he now realised that it would not be won by a small armed band divorced from the vital social issues of the day. He saw that to hold the national question as being above all other issues was to isolate oneself from the Irish people and to make defeat inevitable. He was instrumental in getting Sinn Féin to subsequently drop its abstentionist policy. Seamus remained a revolutionary, maintaining that parliament should be used, but totally rejecting that there was such a thing as a parliamentary road to socialism.

To Seamus Costello lies the honour of defending the socialist line in Republicanism and advocating a return to the traditions of Connolly. He understood that the national question could not be separated from the struggle for socialism and that the armed struggle was worse than useless unless it was linked to the mass struggles of the working class. He saw that it was necessary to combine the struggle for democratic demands and a flexible attitude to the use of parliament and the electoral plane with an uncompromising fight for socialism.

In 1966 he gave the historic oration at the Wolfe Tone commemoration in Bodenstown, which marked the departure to the left of the republican movement, the result of years of discussions within the movement in which he played a key role. He argued in favour of a socialist policy based on the nationalisation of all banks, insurance companies, loan and investment companies.

The IRSP

"Any revolutionary movement that cannot defend its own membership, and cannot demonstrate its capability of defending its own membership, goes out of business anyway. We are in business as a serious revolutionary organisation and we are not going to be put out of business by anybody. The IRSP is organised and it is here to stay." (Seamus Costello, March 1975.)

The period of the 1970s was a turbulent time for the struggle in Ireland, highlighted by a great upsurge in Loyalist sectarian violence in the North and the development of the prison struggle culminating in the 1981 hunger strike, which focused worldwide attention on Ireland. It was also a period of splits and internal feuding within the republican movement. Seamus Costello remained with the Officials during the splits of 1969-70 because he was opposed to splitting the movement. Unfortunately, the conduct of the Stalinist leadership of the Officials made new crises and splits inevitable.

In 1972, the Official IRA had declared an indefinite, unilateral cease-fire. Official Sinn Féin leader, Tomás MacGiolla felt that the movement needed to move away from the armed struggle and instead focus on working class unity between Protestant and Catholic workers in the North; believing that these groups would eventually see a common purpose and rise together against British imperialism. Opponents to this position in the OIRA argued at the 1973 Ard Fheis (national party congress) that this position was unrealistic considering the 400 years of sectarian intransigence in the North, and that instead the armed struggle must be maintained and channelled into a socialist direction.

The Officials began to abandon militant actions in the South and eventually in the North with the cease-fire of 1972. Disillusionment set in the rank and file. Many dropped out, and the clique in the leadership began to orchestrate a witch-hunt of all dissidents. Eventually Seamus Costello was charged with irregularities at the 1973 Ard Fheis and tried by Official Sinn Féin. He was found not guilty. However, the Official IRA tried him on similar charges, with the exact same evidence (ensuring Costello's witnesses didn't turn up) and found him guilty. They dismissed him "with ignominy."

The dominant section of the Officials' leadership was not prepared to allow dissent on the key issues, and were willing to go to any length to suppress it, including force. Finally, on 10th December 1974, led by Costello, the opposition held its own Ard Fheis to declare the formation of the Irish Republican Socialist Party and, at a separate Ard Fheis later that day, founded the Irish National Liberation Army (INLA).

Seamus Costello's idea was to build a strong republican socialist party that would unify the national and class questions as one struggle. He sought to involve the IRSP in all the struggles of the Irish people; trade union work, housing, fisheries, the struggle for women's emancipation, the national question, the struggle of small farmers, tenants, the cultural struggle, sovereignty, the struggle for control over Irish natural resources and the struggle against repression, etc.

Whereas the Provisionals saw national liberation as a primary objective to be achieved before any social programme could be addressed, and the Officials argued social revolution was an essential step before national unification could be considered, the Irish Republican Socialist Movement (IRSM, which combined the IRSP and NILA) returned to the analysis put forward by Connolly, that the struggles for Irish national liberation and for the liberation of the Irish proletariat were inseparable. The IRSM put forward the position that the national liberation struggle was not a step to be climbed before social revolution could be called for, but was simply an aspect of the fight for socialism in Ireland; an essential Irish manifestation of the class war.

This was the correct approach, but unfortunately the party was faced with serious opposition, and not just from the state. The Officials reacted by launching a campaign of assassination, driving the IRSP into hiding. Seamus attempted mediation with the Officials who refused. The feud had seriously affected the growth of the IRSP and stopped most resignations from the Officials. Three IRSP members were dead and scores injured. Finally, Seamus himself fell victim to an assassination. This was a heavy blow. Seamus was a consistent follower of James Connolly, whose writings he had studied assiduously. Nora Connolly said of him:

"He seemed to be the leader who would bring about an organisation such as my father wished to bring about. Of all the politicians and political people with whom I have had conversations, and who called themselves followers of Connolly, he was the only one who truly understood what James Connolly meant when he spoke of his vision of the freedom of the Irish people. In him, I had hoped at last after all these years, a true leader had come, who could and would build an organisation such as James Connolly tried to do."

London digs in its heels

Once its plans for power sharing had failed, the British government battened down the hatches and prepared for a long fight. If they could not get what they wanted through a compromise deal, they were prepared to get it by "other means", to use Clausewitz's famous phrase. Why were they so determined to hold onto the North? At the time of partition, there were powerful economic and strategic considerations at stake. But in the age of intercontinental nuclear missiles the Six Counties no longer had any strategic military importance, whilst from an economic point of view they were a considerable drain. But British imperialism still could not let them go. Why?

It is a mistake to present the relationship between London and the Loyalist forces as a simple black and white question. The relationship was much more complicated than it was in 1922. The British had created a Frankenstein's monster in the shape of sectarianism. And just as Frankenstein could not control his monster, so the British found they could not control the Loyalists. The latter were completely opposed to the unification of Ireland and in 1974 they showed their teeth. It was impossible to get them to accept even such a milk-and-water compromise as a power sharing assembly and a toothless Council of Ireland. They showed themselves to be utterly intransigent, and prepared to go to any lengths to resist, including violence.

The Provisional leadership imagined that they could bomb the Protestants into a united Ireland and compel the British to withdraw. But both assumptions were false, as subsequent events showed. The British were afraid to withdraw because of the chaos that would ensue. They feared that this would lead to open civil war between Catholics and Protestants, with incalculable consequences. Not that they were much concerned about people being killed - on either side. But such a struggle - which would entail terrible atrocities - would inevitably spread to Britain.

The nightmare of sectarian conflict would flare up in cities like Glasgow, Liverpool, Birmingham and London, with widespread terrorism, killings and bombings. This could not be accepted. Therefore, they were stuck with the North, whether they wanted it or not. There was never any question of British imperialism "surrendering to terrorism", as they would put it. That is something the Provisional IRA never understood. The proof is that they embarked on a futile campaign of "armed struggle" for the best part of three decades, leading to a compromise, which they could have had almost from the beginning.

Perhaps in response to the Peace People's campaign, 1977 proved to have the lowest incidents of violence since 1971, with only 112 killed as a result of the war. The lull in the violence was only a temporary respite. London was preparing for an all-out struggle with no holds barred. The British government also stepped up its intelligence-gathering network in the occupied Six Counties, announcing in

1977 that it would computerise information on the residents of the North. Through the computer database, the police and army had access to vast amounts of personal information on virtually all nationalist residents. In 1980 the Army went even farther in eroding the privacy of Six County residents by installing closed-circuit television cameras in the streets of nationalist neighbourhoods in Belfast and Derry. The real viciousness of British imperialism was exposed by its subsequent conduct. Internment without trial, Diplock courts, the hunger strikes and the shoot-to-kill policy revealed the cruel and repressive face that was hidden behind the smiling mask of "democracy".

Part Ten

The prisoners' struggle

Before 1976 Republican prisoners had what was called "special category status," allowing them to be treated as prisoners of war, and providing them with the 'privileges' of POWs, such as those specified in the Geneva Convention. Special category status had been won through a long hunger strike in 1971 by Republican prisoners in Crumlin Road Jail and included:
1. The right to wear their own clothes
2. The right to abstain from penal labour
3. The right to free association
4. The right to normal visits, parcels and educational activities
5. The restoration of remission.

In order to undermine the morale of Republicans, London decided to attack the prisoners. In 1975, the British government began phasing out this status, declaring that anyone convicted after 1st March 1976 was to be treated as a common criminal - an ODC, or "Ordinary Decent Criminal" (!).

The relatives and supporters of the prisoners formed the Relatives' Action Committees to protest against this policy of criminalisation. But the strongest protest came from inside the prisons, from the prisoners themselves. On 15th September 1976, the "blanket protest" began, when Republican prisoners refused to wear prison uniform. By March 1979, a quarter to a third of all sentenced Republican and Republican Socialist prisoners had joined the blanket protest.

Prison guards tried to halt the protest by beating the Blanket Men when they went to shower or use the toilets. In March 1978, the prisoners responded by refusing to leave their cells, no longer washing and using buckets as toilets. The guards then stopped bringing buckets to the cells, the prisoners replied with the "Dirty Protest".

The Relatives' Action Committee's campaign soon drew broad-based support and what had began as a struggle waged within the isolation of the jails, by the prisoners themselves, was developing into a mass movement. On 21st October 1979, the National H-Block/Armagh Committee was established at a conference held in the Andersontown area of Belfast. The new organisation swiftly grew into a mass organisation, which attracted the support of the IRSP, People's Democracy, Sinn Féin, trade unionists, and independent activists of various political stripes in the campaign previously waged almost exclusively by the prisoners' families.

Despite the participation of many of its rank-and-file members, Sinn Féin initially remained somewhat aloof from the growing movement at an organisational level, until the H-Block/Armagh struggle had gained such widespread support that to remain outside it threatened to eclipse their dominance on the Irish Republican political landscape.

The H-Block prisoners prepared to take whatever steps were necessary to win their five demands.

Knowing that the only means to avert a hunger strike was to force Britain to concede the prisoners demands, the activists of the National H-Block Armagh Committee waged a tireless struggle to increase the political pressure on Britain to relent. The mass movement began to score notable successes in exposing the brutality of the authorities. This led to reprisals both by the British imperialists and the Loyalist death squads.

The 1980 Hunger Strike

To attain their five demands, which fundamentally reinstated special category status, the prisoners in the H-Blocks prepared to begin a hunger strike, but on 23rd October 1980, the Northern Ireland Office (NIO) announced that the men would be permitted to wear civilian clothes (the women in Armagh had never lost this right, but had joined the protest to demonstrate their solidarity). However, the concession was a sham, the clothes intended were to be prison-issue civilian clothes, simply exchanging one uniform with another. Outraged over Britain's attempt to deceive them, seven prisoners embarked on a hunger strike.

Both the IRSP and Sinn Féin were opposed to the hunger strike, believing it to be too dangerous a form of protest. They had believed that a broad front protest was the only way to focus worldwide attention on the prison struggle and embarrass London into renewing political status, thereby ending the protest. Despite the H-Block/Armagh Committees having been able to focus international attention on the prisons, the British remained unrelenting, and the prisoners decided, over the objections of their movements outside, that the hunger strike could no longer be delayed, as no other option seemed available to them.

On Sunday 1st March 1981 a new Hunger Strike began with the refusal of

Bobby Sands, then leader of the Provisional Irish Republican Army in the Maze Prison, to take food. It later became clear that the Provo leadership outside the prison was not in favour of a new hunger strike following the outcome of the 1980 strike. The main initiative came from the prisoners themselves. The strike was to last until 3rd October 1981 and was to see 10 Republican prisoners starve themselves to death in support of their protest. The strike led to a heightening of political tensions in the region. It was also to pave the way for the emergence of Sinn Féin (SF) as a major political force in the North.

Thatcher decided that no concessions must be made to the prisoners. With cold, calculated cruelty, she and her clique decided to allow them to die. On Tuesday 3rd March 1981 Humphrey Atkins, then Secretary of State for Northern Ireland, made a statement in the House of Commons in which he said that there would be no political status for prisoners regardless of the hunger strike.

Eventually the leadership of Sinn Féin decided to put forward a candidate for election to highlight the situation, and on 26th March Bobby Sands was nominated. Margaret Thatcher, the then British Prime Minister, paid a visit to the North and denied claims that the constitutional position of Northern Ireland would be threatened by the on-going talks between the British and Irish governments.

Even when Bobby Sands was elected to Westminster in the Fermanagh/South Tyrone by-election, the Thatcher administration remained obdurate. Margaret Thatcher stated: "We are not prepared to consider special category status for certain groups of people serving sentences for crime. Crime is crime is crime, it is not political." The only change it made was to publish proposals to change the Representation of the People Act making it impossible for prisoners to stand as candidates for election to parliament. The hunger strike continued to grow, and on 5th May, Sands became the first of the prisoners to die, after 66 days on hunger strike. He was 26 years old.

This act of wanton cruelty on the part of Thatcher and her government showed not only callousness but also crass stupidity. Far from intimidating the Republican community, it provoked a wave of revulsion and fury. Following the announcement that Bobby Sands had won the Fermanagh/South Tyrone by-election there were celebration parades in Republican areas across the six counties. In Belfast, Cookstown and in Lurgan these celebrations ended in rioting. The announcement of his death sparked riots in many areas of the North, and even in the South.

Other deaths followed. Three members of the Irish National Liberation Army (INLA), Michael Devine, Patsy O'Hara and Keven Lynch, died in the hunger strikes. Proportionate to their numbers, their losses were heavier than those of the Provisional IRA.

On Thursday 7th May 1981 an estimated 100,000 people attended the funeral of Bobby Sands in Belfast. The size of the crowd reflected the impact the hunger strike was having. The hunger strikes continued. Joe McDonnell, then a Provisional Irish Republican Army prisoner in the Maze Prison, joined the hunger strike to take the place of Bobby Sands. On Tuesday 12th May 1981, after 59 days on hunger strike, Francis Hughes (25), a Provisional Irish Republican Army prisoner in the Maze Prison, died. Hughes' death led to a further surge in rioting, particularly in Belfast and Derry. In Dublin a group of 2,000 people tried to break into the British Embassy.

Events were laying the base for a mass movement of protest. Unfortunately, the Provo leadership had no use for the mass movement, except as an auxiliary to the "armed struggle". They still had the delusion that the British army could be forced to pull out by bombing and shooting. The mass movement around the hunger strikes showed enormous promise, but once again the opportunity was thrown away.

Results of the hunger strike

One prisoner after another was allowed to die. Margaret Thatcher, then British Prime Minister, paid a visit to the north where she claimed that the hunger strike was the "last card"' of the Provos. In reality, by taking the stand it did, the British government was acting as the best recruiting sergeant for the Provisionals, who gained a new lease of life from these tragic events. The Provisional Irish Republican Army also stepped up its attacks on members of the security services. The British government had to send in 600 extra British troops. To make matters worse the British government faced extensive international condemnation for the way in which it had handled the hunger strike. The relationship between the British and Irish government was strained to breaking point.

A hunger strike is a desperate measure, which should only be undertaken when there is no other alternative. The death of cadres in the prisons is a very high price to pay. There also is a limit to how far a hunger strike can go. This hunger strike finally ended in October 1981, when those Republican prisoners who had been still refusing food decided to end their fast. The prisoners took their decision when it became clear that each of their families would ask for medical intervention to save their lives. Ten Republican prisoners had died inside the Maze Prison as a result of the strike. Another 62 people were killed in demonstrations and clashes with the police.

Despite the high cost in lives, the Republican movement had achieved a huge propaganda victory over the British government and had obtained a great deal of international sympathy. More importantly, the hunger strike shook masses of people in the 26 Counties out of their lethargy, and brought huge crowds out onto the streets of the North. The hunger strike also won large numbers of new recruits to the PIRA and INLA, as well as Sinn Féin and the IRSP. International support organisations for the Irish national liberation struggle sprang up where they had not been before, and grew where they had already existed. The struggle also got an echo in Britain. In September 1981 the British Labour Party's annual conference passed a motion committing the party to "campaign actively" for a United Ireland by consent.

The hunger strike of 1981 had very important and far-reaching consequences and proved to be one of the key turning points of "the Troubles". The heroism of the hunger strikers had had a big effect, and the Thatcher government was forced to make concessions. On 6th October 1981 James Prior, then Secretary of State for Northern Ireland, announced a series of measures which went a long way to meeting many aspects of the prisoners' five demands.

Prior announced a number of changes in prison policy, one of which would allow prisoners to wear their civilian clothes at all times. This was one of the five key demands that had been made at the start of the hunger strike. Prior also announced other changes: free association would be allowed in neighbouring wings of each H-Block, in the exercise areas and in recreation rooms; an increase in the number of visits each prisoner would be entitled to; and up to 50 per cent of lost remission would be restored. The issue of prison work was not resolved at this stage but there were indications that this issue too would be addressed.

The obstinate stupidity of Thatcher had the most negative results for British imperialism. They had helped the Provisional IRA. Support for Sinn Féin was demonstrated in the two by-elections and eventually led to the emergence of Sinn Féin as a significant political force. The British government now feared that Sinn Féin would overtake the Social Democratic and Labour Party (SDLP) as the main representative of the Catholic population of the North. This was a key reason for the Anglo-Irish Agreement of November 1985.

Armalite or ballot box?

Having failed to crush the movement by brutal repression, London tried a different tactic: to entangle the PIRA in parliamentary politics. In this they were enthusiastically encouraged by the bourgeoisie of the South. Garret FitzGerald, then Taoiseach (Irish Prime Minister), held talks with Margaret Thatcher, then British Prime Minister, in London. As a result of the meeting it was decided to establish the Anglo-Irish Inter-Governmental Council, which would act as forum for meetings between the two governments.

There were now serious differences over tactics in the ranks of the Provisionals. One wing of the Sinn Féin leadership was more inclined towards parliamentarianism while others favoured the continuation of the armed struggle. The result was an uncomfortable compromise, which went under the name of the "Armalite and ballot box" tactic. After the hunger strike, Sinn Féin began fielding candidates for local councils and the European parliament. In the autumn of 1981 Sinn Féin held its Ard Fheis in Dublin. Danny Morrison, then editor of *An Phoblacht*, gave a speech in which he addressed the issue of the party taking part in future elections:

"Who here really believes we can win the war through the ballot box? But will anyone here object if, with a ballot paper in one hand and the Armalite in the other, we take power in Ireland?"

This tactic was intended to paper over the cracks in the Provos. But British imperialism was not willing to play games. It decided to crush the PIRA, fighting with no holds barred. Immediately following the hunger strike, the British tried several tactics to break political activists and those under arms against the occupation. The attempt of the Provisionals to renew their bombing campaign in the 1980s was met with a ferocious response on the part of the security services, involving the notorious shoot-to-kill tactics. These were used mostly against members of the PIRA and INLA, but on occasion, civilians were also killed. In an official investigation, the killings of six men were examined, three were in the PIRA, two in the INLA, and one was a young civilian. A chief constable from England, John Stalker, was appointed to head the investigation. He was stonewalled by the RUC, and allegations of impropriety were made against him. The "shoot-to-kill" investigation became "Stalker-gate" after he was removed from the investigation.

It came as no great surprise to anyone that the RUC and British Army were found innocent of any deliberate attempt to kill PIRA and INLA members. In a separate case, the European Convention on Human Rights ruled that Britain should be taken before the European Court of Human Rights, and tried for the deaths of Provo volunteers and staff officers Mairead Farrell, Seán Savage and Danny McCann, known as the Gibraltar 3. The trio were assassinated by the British Army on Gibraltar, after which the British government attempted a cover-up, stating that a bomb was found in their car. When this failed, Thatcher's people tried to blame the Spanish security forces, who refused to be the fall guys for the cold-blooded murder of the three. Again, the British courts found those involved in the killings innocent of wrongdoing.

The full extent of the involvement of the British security services in these events is only now coming to light. The collusion of the British state with loyalist murder gangs, the killing of lawyer Pat Finucane and many others, has been exposed in recent times. Even more so the allegations of the existence of an agent reporting to British intelligence at the highest levels of the PIRA, the Stakeknife affair, has dealt the Provos a further blow.

By 1993, elected representatives of both Sinn Féin and the SDLP increasingly became targets for attack. The British organised the wholesale arrest of members of the Republican and Republican Socialist movements, on the word of a "reformed terrorist," that is, a paid perjurer. Most times, these "supergrasses" ("grass" being slang for informer) would be given a list of names and "crimes" to sign. Although eventually many of these cases were thrown out on appeal, they had a demoralising effect on activists. As a smaller organisation, the Irish Republican Socialist Movement was particularly hard hit. Unlike during the hunger strike, a mass, organised opposition to the informers tactic failed to materialise, in part due to Sinn Féin's insistence on political domination of any mass group.

To boycott or not to boycott?

Sinn Féin began its foray into electoral politics as a direct result of the hunger strike campaign. In 1983, Gerry Adams, Sinn Féin president, was elected as MP for West Belfast, and held the seat until April 1992. Sinn Féin members were elected to county and city councils in the North and South. The party even went so far as to restructure its Cummain (branches) on the basis of electoral districts. In 1986, after much debate over several years, Sinn Féin dropped its policy of abstentionism in Dáil Eireann. Ironically this had been the ostensible reason for the split from the Officials in late 1969/early 1970, though the real reasons were more profound.

The decision to abandon the abstentionist line was a correct one. As a general rule of thumb, a revolutionary party only has the right to boycott elections when it is in a position to offer something superior - i.e. soviet power, a genuine workers' democracy. Otherwise it is duty bound to participate in elections, the extent depending on the means at their disposal - this does not necessarily involve standing candidates, but not standing is not the same as a boycott - as a means of reaching the masses. To refuse to participate would mean the party boycotting itself. However, in this case, this reflected a change in principle as well as tactics. The dropping of abstentionism led to a split in Sinn Féin, when hard-line abstentionists walked out of the Ard Fheis and formed Republican Sinn Féin, a political party with little politics, which supported armed struggle, but had no army. The PIRA had declared its support for the new order in a convention held several weeks before the Ard Fheis.

In 1982, elections were held for a new assembly in the North. The British tried to bring in "rolling devolution," but the attempt failed utterly. The Unionist parties supported the Northern Ireland Assembly, but the nationalist community was divided over the issue. The body would have very limited power, as a sop to the Loyalists. The bourgeois nationalists of the SDLP supported the assembly, and sought election with the intention of taking seats. The IRSP advocated a boycott, and initially, Sinn Féin supported the idea.

After the SDLP announced it would run, Sinn Féin changed its mind, deciding to also field candidates, but on an abstentionist platform. The IRSP, with the Irish Independence Party, continued to advocate boycotting, but if voting, to vote Sinn Féin. During the election campaign, the INLA engaged in a bombing campaign to disrupt the election. The bombing campaign was criticised by Sinn Féin. The whole mess came to an ignoble end after several years, when the Unionists pulled out over the Anglo-Irish Agreement, and the only party left participating was the SDLP.

Part Eleven

The Good Friday Agreement

The contradictions in Sinn Féin's electoral policies became sharper during the 1992 Westminster election. Sinn Féin president Gerry Adams several times called for UN intervention in the North! This was a far cry from the "Ourselves Alone" days of Sinn Féin in the early 1970s. *In other words, Adams and other leaders of Sinn Féin had lost all confidence in their ability to defeat British imperialism and achieve a united Ireland through the armed struggle.*

In private Adams and McGuiness recognised that they had been defeated, and that a radical change of course was necessary. But instead of making a serious self-criticism and concluding that it was necessary to return to the ideas and methods of James Connolly, they moved in the direction of reformism and parliamentarianism. The Sinn Féin leadership was now desperate to be involved in any talks or negotiations with London. They clung to the illusion that this might eventually lead to the withdrawal of British troops from the North, and even possible reunification. This was a dream, as subsequent events have shown. But what was increasingly clear was that the campaign of bombing and shooting had not even dented the determination of British imperialism to hang onto the Six Counties.

Ard Fheisanna began to emphasize the separation between Sinn Féin and the PIRA, repeatedly stating that Sinn Féin is "not a party of violence". Yet the Provos continued their campaign in the Six Counties and England. In 1992, the PIRA engaged in a Christmas bombing campaign, and set off bombs in England throughout the winter of 1992/93, however, a ceasefire was called for 72 hours, beginning on Christmas day. The INLA, in a symbolic action on the first day of the ceasefire, fired upon an observation post, demonstrating its distinct presence in the national liberation struggle.

In the autumn of 1993, Sinn Féin drafted a proposal for a peace settlement jointly with the SDLP. Details of the document have been closely guarded, but the

Dublin government, to which it was presented, passed it along to the British government for review. In late 1993 it was revealed that Britain's Tory government had been engaged in secret negotiations with the Provisionals for some time.

What we wrote at the time

Those negotiations bore fruit in 1994 with the declaration of an unconditional ceasefire by the Provisional IRA. Following the ceasefire Ted Grant wrote an analysis of these developments which is well worth reading again today. The following extracts do not really do justice to the pamphlet as a whole but hopefully provide a flavour of what the Marxists wrote at the time:

"The declaration of an unconditional ceasefire by the IRA on the 31st August represents a crushing defeat for the policy of individual terrorism. For 25 years the IRA waged an armed struggle against British imperialism, with the declared aim of driving out the British army and achieving the unification of Ireland. Now, after a generation of conflict, the goal of a united Ireland is further away than ever…

"In the first place it is necessary to place the responsibility for the problems of Ireland where they belong – at the door of British imperialism… However, the history of Ireland is a striking demonstration of the correctness of the theory of permanent revolution… All the heroic exertions of the Irish people were betrayed by the bourgeois nationalist leaders…

"At each stage of the Irish liberation struggle, the national question has been inextricably linked to social problems. At bottom it is a class question. The emancipation of the Irish people can only be won through the emancipation of the working class, which has no interest in any form of national or religious oppression…

"The whole history of the struggle in Northern Ireland demonstrates that the only way to solve the problem is on the basis of a class programme. The moment you abandon the class standpoint you enter on the slippery slope to disaster. All the other tendencies on the Left bowed to the pressure of nationalism, with predictable results. The leaders of Sinn Féin, while paying 'lip-service' to a socialist Ireland in the dim and distant future, insisted that the struggle for socialism be postponed until the 'question of the border' was settled. In this they have been mimicked by all the sectarian groups in Britain, who have played a despicable role, acting as cheerleaders of the IRA for the last 25 years, with not the slightest pretence of a class position…

"After 25 years the strategy of the IRA lies in ruins. The cause of Irish unification has been set back for decades by the legacy of fear and hatred between the two communities as a result. Thus the alleged 'realism' of the nationalists has achieved precisely the opposite result to what was intended. The prior condition for a successful struggle against British imperialism is to achieve the united action of the working class, cutting across the sectarian divisions of religion and nationality. This can never be achieved on the basis of nationalism. The only realistic policy is therefore a revolutionary class policy aimed at the overthrow of capitalist rule north and south of the border and in Britain…

"So after all these years the British army will not be withdrawn, the Unionist veto will not be abolished, and the border will not disappear! So what was it all in aid of? So many sacrifices, so many dead, and for what? What concessions have been gained? … Probably Whitehall will come up with some new plan for power sharing. They may even succeed this time in setting up an Assembly, which they failed to do in 1973-4.

"It is quite likely that there is a secret deal concerning the release of Republican prisoners. It would be almost impossible for Adams and McGuiness to sell any deal to their members which did not include that. However, the British will demand as a prior condition that the Provisionals hand in their arms. Since they have a huge arsenal, they will probably hand over part of it, and keep the rest 'for a rainy day'. It is clear that the majority of the leaders of the IRA have despaired of achieving anything from the 'armed struggle' and therefore would be prepared to do this.

"What is ruled out is any possibility of a secret deal to bring about a united Ireland, at least for the foreseeable future…

"No matter how they twist and turn, no matter how many times they re-write the laws and the constitution, it will not stop the rot. An elected Assembly in Northern Ireland would be no answer. How could it solve the problem of unemployment, or build enough houses for all? The crisis of the social system will continue to gnaw at the bowels of society, spawning more frustration, crime, and sectarian madness. The only way is to put an end to the root cause of all our ills, the system of rent, interest and profit…

"Such a perspective seems difficult? But haven't we had enough of so-called 'easy' solutions in Ireland, above all for the last 25 years?… To all the sceptics and cynics who cast doubt upon the ability of the Irish workers to unite to fight for their emancipation as a class, sweeping aside the sectarian muck, we shall reply in the words of the finest son of the Irish and British working class, James Connolly:

"'As we have again and again pointed out, the Irish question is a social question, the whole age long fight of the Irish people against their oppressors resolves itself in the last analysis into a fight for the mastery of the means of life, the sources of production in Ireland…Yet plain as this is to us today, it is undeniable that for two hundred years at least all Irish political movements ignored this fact, and were conducted by men who did not look below the political surface. These men, to arouse the passions of the people invoked the memory of social wrongs, such as evictions and famines, but for these wrongs proposed only political remedies, such as changes in taxation or transference of the seat of government (class rule) from one country to another. Hence they accomplished nothing because the political remedies proposed were unrelated to the social subjection at the root of the matter. The revolutionists of the past were wiser, the Irish socialists are wiser today. In their movement the North and the South will again clasp hands, again will it be demonstrated as in '98, that the pressure of a common exploitation can make enthusiastic rebels out of a Protestant working class, earnest champions of civil and religious liberty out of Catholics, and out of both a united Social Democracy.'" (Ted Grant, *Ireland After the Ceasefire, 1994*)

A Reactionary agreement

In 1998 the Good Friday Agreement was signed. This was a reactionary agreement made between British imperialism and the leadership of the Provisionals. Like all past agreements it is doomed to failure. It has served to illustrate the desperation of the leadership of the Provos. After thirty years of bloody armed struggle, they come out with their hands empty. Adams and McGuinness put on suits and enter Stormont as ministers, having substituted "constitutional" politics for a militant anti-imperialist perspective.

This result could have been foreseen. British imperialism had no intention of allowing the Provisional IRA to succeed. It had no choice in the matter. The irony is that British imperialism no longer has any real interest in hanging onto the North. It has become a huge financial drain and a serious political and military embarrassment. But London cannot now disengage from the North. They are hoist by their own petard.

From an economic point of view, possession of the Six Counties is not a plus but a huge minus for Britain. It costs them an enormous amount to maintain control of the North, between the cost of a vast security operation, social security and other subsidies to an economically depressed area. In point of fact, the British capitalists would be pleased to get rid of Northern Ireland. They attempted to do so in the 1960s when they started negotiations between O' Neil and Lemass. But here the dialectic of history played a trick on them. The Frankenstein monster of Protestant sectarianism revolted and undermined the plans of the British and Irish bourgeois.

Therefore, the British imperialists were determined to crush the Provos by every means at their disposal. Despite the occasional spectacular action, the PIRA was really defeated, although nobody is prepared to admit such a thing.

The truth had begun to dawn on the leadership. Eventually, people like Adams and McGuinness understood the hopelessness of the position. They saw that even if the PIRA continued fighting for another 30 years, the outcome would be exactly the same.

An estimated 90 percent voted "Yes" to the Agreement. This is hardly surprising. The masses are tired of so many years of fruitless violence with no end in sight. No other perspective is offered to them. But in practice the illusions in the Agreement (such as they are) will not last long. After the Agreement nothing fundamental has changed. Britain's armed groupings such as the RUC (now the Police Service of Northern Ireland) and the RIR, in conjunction with their Loyalists militias, still remain active and intact despite limited reform. The working people on both sides of the sectarian divide have gained very little. Under conditions of capitalist crisis, with more unemployment and cuts on the way, the horrible spectre of sectarian strife can result in a renewal of violence, bloodshed and mayhem.

Reformism and Parliamentarism

The whole history of Ireland shows that it is impossible to eradicate the national movement through state repression. But the history of the last 30 years has also shown the impossibility of achieving the goal of a united Ireland on the basis of this kind of "armed struggle". Since they had no intention of leading any other kind of struggle - i.e., a mass struggle of a united working class which could really challenge imperialism - their next move was predictable. The leaders of the Provisional IRA and Sinn Féin drew the conclusions and in effect went over to the politics of reformism and parliamentarism. Minor concessions have been made by British imperialism but nothing fundamental has changed. *About the aim of a united Ireland nothing is said. But this was the declared goal of the PIRA for the last 30 years of armed struggle for which so many lives were lost.*

The repeated suspension of "power-sharing" and the continual crises of the devolved institutions demonstrate that the whole set-up is extremely fragile and unsound. The present unstable truce will eventually break down - it is breaking down already. And then what? A return of the old vicious spiral of tit-for-tat sectarian murders, bombings, arrests, detention without trial and internment: the infernal logic of action - reaction, the loss of innocent life, the physical destruction of yet another generation of Irish youth; a further deepening of the sectarian divide?

The leaders of the Provisionals have gained a few paltry ministerial portfolios (except that Stormont is closed down more often than not) and some so-called concessions that are not worth the paper they are written on. Nothing has been solved for either Catholics or Protestants. On the contrary, the situation has been made far worse. With over three thousand deaths; the destruction of a whole generation of Irish youth; the splitting of the population of the North into two hostile camps; a terrible legacy of sectarian bitterness. And with what result? Has the border question been solved? Let us speak clearly: *After three decades of so-called armed struggle, the cause of Irish reunification is further away today than at any other time.*

This is the terrible legacy of decades of individual terrorism and the total lack of any class or socialist perspective. True, there was a serious division in the past between Catholics and Protestants in Northern Ireland. But now in place of division we have a yawning abyss. Yet none of this would have been necessary if Connolly's ideas and methods had prevailed.

Ireland and the British Left

In its early days, the British Labour Party supported Home Rule for Ireland - a fact that was commented on favourably by Connolly, who was always an internationalist. But now they are completely degenerate. The right wing leaders of the British Labour Party have for decades acted as the faithful spokesmen of British imperialism. They have been more slavish to imperialism than even the Tories. However, the development of class struggle in Britain and Ireland will cut across this and undermine the right wing. This process has already begun in the unions in Britain, where the Blairite right wing leaders have been emptied out and replaced by the Left.

In 1969 most of the British Left - including all those who later supported the "Troops Out" Movement - *were completely in favour of sending in the British army*. That was true of the Labour Left, the Communist Party and the SWP. They argued that the army was being sent to defend the Catholics. An honourable exception was the Marxist tendency in the British Labour Party, at that time grouped around the *Militant*, which came down firmly against the sending of British troops to the North. They wrote at the time: "The call made for the entry of British troops will turn to vinegar in the mouths of some of the civil rights leaders. The troops have been sent in to impose a solution in the interests of British and Ulster big business." (*Militant*, September 1969.)

At the Labour Party conference in the autumn of 1969 our comrades moved Emergency Resolution No. 2, which states:

"This Conference declares its opposition to the sectarian attacks on the Derry and Belfast workers which took place in August of this year.

"It condemns this action on the part of the Royal Ulster Constabulary, sections of the B Specials and Paisleyite thugs.

"It affirms its support for those sections of the Irish Labour Movement, particularly the Derry Labour Party, which have attempted to unite both Protestant and Catholic workers against the common enemy, the capitalist class, whether they be Orange or Green, and calls upon the trade unions of Ireland to contain the sectarian terror by the organisation of Joint Defence Committees comprising of both Protestant and Catholic workers.

"Conference believes that British imperialism and its supporters in Ireland have deliberately used and helped to maintain the religious sectarianism in order to ensure its investments in both North and South Ireland on the basis of the policy of 'divide and rule'."

The movers of the resolution stated in the debate:

"We have got to back up our comrades in Northern Ireland, we have got to demand, as they do, the withdrawal of British troops. British troops have never acted in the interests of the working class in any country."

However, the rest of the British Left played a lamentable role. Having supported the sending of British troops to the North (allegedly to help the Catholics), they then performed a 180-degree somersault and uncritically backed the bombing campaign of the Provisional IRA. From the safety of their Hampstead flats, they cheered the "armed struggle", although none of them were in any personal danger. A particularly pernicious role was played for decades by the ultra-left sects in Britain and internationally on the question of Ireland. These ladies and gentlemen interpreted "support for the national liberation struggle" to mean *uncritical support for the Provisional IRA*.

The Provisionals, who were a right wing tendency, cynically used the services of these groups, while behind their backs they treated them with well-deserved contempt. In their enthusiasm to back the Provos, the sects forget the little "detail" that the Provisional IRA was set up in 1969 on the basis of guns and money supplied by the Blaney-Houghey wing of Fianna Fail. Although they played no role in the movement of the masses in the North in 1968-9, they were able to take it over because they possessed the organisation and the arms that the aroused youth of the North were looking for.

Bourgeois trend

Despite all their "revolutionary" demagogy and talk of "armed struggle", from the standpoint of ideology the Provos were - and remain - a *bourgeois right wing* trend in Republicanism. In the past they even burned Marxist books. They led the majority of the movement for 30 years along a road that has finally ended nowhere, and then signed an Agreement that completely abandoned the cause of reunification for the sake of ministerial positions. Though they swore by Lenin in every other sentence, the sectarian fans of the Provos did considerable damage to the Irish cause in Britain and internationally. They demonstrated a complete lack of understanding of both the national liberation struggle and of the Leninist position towards it. In addition through their words and their deeds they damaged the perception of Marxism in the eyes of activists in Ireland.

Having applauded the Provo's counterproductive bombing campaigns, which contributed to the sectarian divide and completely alienated British workers, they were left with their mouths hanging open when the Provo leadership signed up to the Good Friday Agreement. The Irish workers can do without such "allies". Instead we should look towards building links between British and Irish trade unionists - in struggle against the bosses, our common enemies - especially at the level of the shop stewards and the rank and file activists. After all, as the shift to the Left in the British trade unions shows, the rank and file workers are not the same as their leaders!

There were always people on the Left in Britain who opposed imperialism from a consistent revolutionary class standpoint. The Marxist tendency in the British workers' movement has a proud record on Ireland. We were the only consistent ones who opposed the sending in of British troops in 1969, and moved a resolution at the Labour Party conference on these lines in the autumn of 1969. The British Marxist tendency now represented by *Socialist Appeal* and the Marxist.com website also opposed the Good Friday Agreement as a deception and a betrayal. The supporters of the international Marxist tendency offer their hand in friendship to the workers and youth of Ireland in the struggle against capitalism and imperialism. It is of the utmost importance to us that our ideas are no longer kept a secret from the best elements in the Republican movement. Once our real ideas are known it will soon become clear that we are talking the same language and fighting for the same things.

Part Twelve

A change of course is needed!

Although we have many criticisms of the methods used by the Provisional IRA, we do not mean to disparage the heroism and good intentions of those who, out of impatience and lack of perspective, resorted to what they understood to be the armed struggle against British imperialism. How could one not grieve at the long list of brave young people who have lost their lives fighting for a cause they held dear enough to make the ultimate sacrifice? But we fervently believe that these efforts and sacrifices could and should have been put to better and more effective use.

The argument about good intentions cuts no ice. It is well known that the way to hell is paved with good intentions. And wrong tactics have produced a hellish situation for the working class and youth of the Six Counties. We must judge the effectiveness of men's actions not on the basis of their intentions, but only on the results achieved. From this point of view, we are convinced that, if they are honest, the advocates of the kind of armed struggle pursued in the past period must agree with us that the results achieved bear no relation whatever to the losses incurred.

In the First World War, the generals on both sides sent millions of brave young men to their deaths in futile offensives, which achieved nothing except maybe a few hundred yards of muddy ground. Yet anyone who raised their voice in protest against this futile slaughter was immediately branded a coward and a traitor and even sentenced to be shot. Nowadays, with the wisdom of hindsight, those who had the courage to question an insane tactic have been rehabilitated, whereas the generals stand condemned. Moreover, the finest military minds that realised the worthlessness of the old tactics and worked out new and more efficient ones, were the ones who really advanced the science of warfare and prepared the tactics of the Second World War.

It is just the same with us. When it is clear to anyone capable of thinking that the old methods have failed, surely it is incumbent upon us to speak openly and without fear? Is it not abundantly clear that the time has come to demand a *change of course*? Yet, sadly, every attempt to get the Republican movement to re-examine its tactics and strategy in the light of experience is met with a howl of protest, dark accusations of cowardice and treachery, and even worse things. In order to silence criticism and stifle debate, unscrupulous appeals are made to dead comrades, who, being dead, cannot speak for themselves. To this demagogy, we reply: it is precisely out of respect for our dead that we feel the urgent obligation to speak out and say what is. For what would really be cowardice, what would really be an insult to those who so selflessly gave their lives for the Republican cause, would be to hush up the mistakes, crimes and blunders that have led us to the state we now find ourselves in. For then those who died would certainly have died in vain.

Thomas "Ta" Power

The Republican socialists however, have embarked on just such a serious discussion and criticism of Republicanism, of the movement's history, strategy and tactics, in order to chart a new course for the struggle. The conclusions drawn in the document written by Thomas "Ta" Power represent a serious attempt to draw lessons from the history of the movement, above all the need for politics, political ideas and political struggle to be placed at the top of the agenda. As the introduction to the document points out: "The essay called for the armed aspect of the movement to subordinate itself to the political direction of the party. In Ireland, where physical force has been inseparably linked to the concept of republicanism for centuries, and where the party, if it existed at all, was usually no more than an apparatus through which the army spoke, this was a virtually unheard of concept."

Perhaps even more remarkable is the fact that the document was written while Ta Power was an imprisoned member of the INLA. In January 1987 Ta Power was shot and killed by representatives of the so-called Irish People's Liberation Organisation - the IPLO. The only purpose for the existence of this group it seems was to try to destroy the Republican Socialist Movement.

Ta made a careful study of Marxist ideas while in prison, and the influence of these ideas is clear in the document. The primacy of politics in the movement is the starting point to which must be added the importance of internal democracy and a list of eight other organisational conclusions drawn from the previous experience of the movement. These are highly instructive. In reality they represent the skeleton of the structure of a genuinely revolutionary party.

Along with an honest history of the movement, the document seeks to point the way forward for republican socialists. Not just in its organisational analysis but above all the politics contained in this document represent an important contribution to that process. For example the document draws the following conclusions on the nature of the struggle in Ireland:

"What forces can bring the national question to a successful conclusion? Only the working class. The leading capitalist parties in the 6 and the 26 counties have no interest in solving the national question, but rather in crushing those trying to resolve it.

"Marxism tells us that before we can properly solve a problem, before we can work out a plan of action, etc., that we must first analyse the given process, i.e., that we must identify the basic contradiction which is inherent in it and which give rise to its development, and from which everything else springs.

"The basic contradiction in society is between the relations of production, i.e., socialised production by the working class and private appropriation by the capitalist class.

"It is impossible to bring about 'fundamental change' unless the basic contradiction is tackled and changed.

"Therefore we have to ask now: why, if we're Marxists, do we neglect this? This fundamental of Marxism! Why do we fail to act accordingly? Marx, Lenin, etc., confronted all fundamentals in a courageous, merciless, ruthless manner. Why do we fail to do so? Is it inherent in us? Are we up to this task? Do we lack the courage and maturity to do this? Are we amateurs and not professionals? We know the lessons of history, we know the mistakes, and we either act accordingly or collapse. Salvation lies in clarity and the courage to implement change!"

Having outlined the central role of the working class, and the socialist tasks of the revolution, to deal with the fundamental contradiction in society which lies at the root of all other problems, the document also explains that this struggle is not to proceed in "stages" with the socialist revolution postponed until after national liberation has been achieved, but instead, as Connolly had always argued, the struggles for national and social emancipation are inseparably bound together, and both are tasks confronting the working class.

"When outlining earlier in the programme the front for a constitutional change etc., we don't see this as the so-called 'stages' process in which, for example, once we have got rid of the British we will go through a period of capitalist rule, democratisation, etc...

"The whole question of a constitutional conference will be to debate the question of power. Anyhow, this will depend on the correlation of forces. Within and outside the country it will open up a period of intense struggle between two fundamental camps.

"Ireland continuing as a dependent capitalist country controlled and dominated by imperialism, and of firmly establishing our sovereignty and building a revolutionary socialist state.

"There is no middle ground between the two; there cannot be any middle road. The battle may be delayed or postponed but it must be fought eventually! We must be under no illusions about the utmost clarity if we are to confront it and be successful.

"In Connolly's words: *'we cannot conceive of a free Ireland with a subject working class, we cannot conceive of a suject Ireland with a free working class'*.

"We come once more to the role of the revolutionary party, which is absolutely essential if we are to be successful. Without that clear guide role, without a revolutionary ideology, without an analysis of the forces arranged against us, without the application of the correct tactics and strategy the struggle will fail."

This question of building a revolutionary party, and what tactics and strategy such a party should adopt is a central theme of the document.

"A revolutionary party must have a revolutionary ideology, an ideology that enables us to analyse the world, the motive force at work in the world, and plan a campaign based on the analysis.

"A campaign that is consistent, principled, and bold in its implementation, maxims as a guide to action is ideology; it represents the historical interests of the working class, which through the medium of a revolutionary party, aims to overthrow the capitalist order and begin the construction of communism.

"There is no easy road to a socialist republic, no short cuts, we must strive towards uniting and politicising the working class no matter what obstacles confront us in our task, for we cannot win our struggle without the working class.

"We cannot make the revolution without them, without their active participation in a united and politically conscious manner. We need to be able to bring to the fore their deeply felt aspirations and social needs. To bring to the fore their underlying anti-imperialist sentiment, showing up the class nature of the Irish state, establishment parties, etc., in acting to repress, jail and crush their people in order to protect British rule in Ireland.

"We must be able to inject into the struggle, or rather, call forth from the people the values and ideals of solidarity, self-sacrifice, non-sectarianism, unity and internationalism, etc., values that transcend our own individual existence, that lead to greater awareness, greater participation, and greater aliveness in oneself. We must be somehow able to grip the mass of people if we are to change the world...

"Finally we must constantly review, criticise and self-criticise all aspects of our actions, policies, tactics, etc., keep appraising the whole situation and keep striving to raise the class consciousness, spirit, and capacity to fight and win of the working class."

The tasks which are placed in front of the republican socialist movement in these lines are crystal clear. The building of a revolutionary party of the working class, on the bedrock of Marxist ideas, a party that explains those ideas in a clear way to workers; that constantly strives to raise the consciousness of the working class; and strives for the unity of the working class on all occasions. A party built on internal democracy, on clear ideas, and on internationalism.

These are the conclusions which Ta and other republican socialists drew from an honest appraisal of the development of their movement over a period of decades. The bourgeois and petit bourgeois trend in Republicanism, meanwhile, is incapable of such an analysis. Not only would such conclusions be alien to them, they would certainly not be willing to admit mistakes and errors, they would not even be willing to discuss such matters.

The leaders of the Provisionals have understood nothing from the history of the last 30 years. Understandably, they do not want a democratic and open debate, because the rank and file would begin to draw uncomfortable conclusions. In the ranks of the Provisionals there were many sincere and heroic individuals. But the class nature of the movement is ultimately determined by the leadership, its class outlook, programme and policies. The Provo leadership, although it included some ex-lefts like Gerry Adams, have consistently displayed their hostility to socialism in deeds. But the whole history of the national liberation struggle in Ireland shows that neither the bourgeoisie nor the petty bourgeoisie are capable of leading the movement to victory and the history of the last thirty years is no exception to this rule. In the end, their policies and tactics have proven to be bankrupt.

This sad truth is beginning to dawn on rank and file Republicans, most of whom are ordinary working people and youths who are fighting for a better life. There is a ferment in the Republican movement, which will mean that many good militants will now be open to the ideas of socialism. This is the only way to save the movement and lead it onto a new and higher level, having drawn all the necessary political and organisational conclusions form past mistakes. *It is not enough to lament the past and ask forgiveness for old mistakes. It is necessary to learn from the past in order not to repeat the same mistakes in the future.*

The question of armed struggle

"To imagine that we can establish a republic solely by constitutional means is utter folly". (Seamus Costello)

"The road to hell is paved with good intentions. The burning question - the priority for us is to build a revolutionary party - as Lenin said about the Social Revolutionaries, 'their terrorism is not connected in any way with work among the masses, or together with the masses. It distracts our very scanty organisational

forces from their difficult and by no means complete task of organising a revolutionary party.' " (Ta Power)

The question of armed struggle has a long history in Ireland. A people or a class that is not prepared to fight for its freedom, arms in hand, does not deserve to be free. Despite all the talk of the pacifists, history shows that in the end all serious questions are determined by force, whether in the struggle between nations or in the struggle between classes. Marxists do not require any lessons on this particular topic. Let it not be forgotten that the main force behind the Easter Rising was Connolly's Citizens' Army. Sinn Féin played no role at all, while the middle class leaders of the Irish Volunteers treacherously stabbed the Rising in the back. In the end, yet again, it was the "men of no property" who were in the first rank of the fighters for Irish freedom.

Yes, we understand only too well the significance of armed struggle. For us it is a question of ABC. *But after ABC there are other letters in the alphabet.* To reduce everything to the question of arms is clearly a mistake. The working class should certainly learn how to use arms, but it must also learn many other things, including when to use arms and when not to use them. The class struggle has many weapons and many different forms of struggle: the strike, the general strike, mass demonstrations, boycotts, the parliamentary struggle, etc. It must learn how to make use of all these methods to further its cause. Moreover, different methods will be appropriate for different period and contexts.

The methods of struggle of the working class are different to the methods of other classes, like the peasantry, the petty bourgeois and lumpen-proletariat. Its methods are collective methods, reflecting its role in production. The strike and the general strike involve mass participation and democratic discussion and decision-making. It is a real school for socialism, leading to a raising of class consciousness. By contrast, the method of a so-called "armed struggle" when it is waged by a minority in the name of the working class and behind the backs of the latter is worse than useless. It is not only ineffective but actually counterproductive, since it tends to lower the level of consciousness of the class and undermine its confidence in itself.

Connolly's Citizens' Army was based on the working class and the labour movement. It was organised on class lines. Its perspective was not just an Irish republic, *but an Irish Workers' Republic.* That was a cause which working people could identify with! That was a cause for which they were prepared to fight and die. Therefore, the Citizens' Army had nothing in common with the Provisional IRA, either in its aims, policies or methods. In reality, the three things cannot be separated. The policies of the proletarian party flow from its aims and the methods also. The working class cannot borrow its methods of struggle from other classes, like the petty bourgeoisie and the peasantry. The proletariat differs from all other classes in society in its role in production. It is the only class with an instinctive collectivist consciousness that comes from its role in social production.

Before the Russian revolution, the Bolsheviks used to call the terrorists of Narodnaya Volya "liberals with a bomb". This is now seen to be literally true. Adams and MacGuinness cast aside the armalite and the bomb and take up their ministerial portfolios with the ease of a man passing from the second to the first class carriage of a train. What has all of this achieved? *They achieved the exact opposite of what was intended.* What policy do these Republicans now pursue in their assembly (when it meets)? They pursue a capitalist policy not in the interests of workers from any background.

Individual Terrorism

We are against individual terrorism. But we are not pacifists. The attempt to counterpoise pacifism to the tactics of the Provisional IRA inevitably ended in a farce, although there were undoubtedly many sincere people involved in the various Peace movements. Like individual terrorism, pacifism also achieves the opposite to what it intends. Weakness invites aggression. We are in favour of making use of all the legal opportunities open to us. We are not against participating in parliament. We do not advocate violence, but we are also realists and we understand that no ruling class in history has ever given up its power and privileges without a fight. We are not pacifists but the notion that the armed struggle has an independent significance, divorced from the mass movement, is entirely false.

The organised labour movement must conquer one position at a time: in the workplace, in the housing estates, in the local councils and the Assembly. By strengthening its organisations, it is preparing the ground for the final goal: the socialist revolution. The armed struggle is part and parcel of that struggle, but it is *only* a part, not the whole. Among a section of the movement there has been a tendency to overestimate the independent power of the gun. This is a serious mistake. A moment's reflection should suffice to convince us that if this were really the case, no revolution in history could ever have succeeded, since the state always possesses much greater military resources than the revolutionaries. The reason why revolutions succeed is not because they possess enormous military strength, but because behind the revolution stand the masses. It is only the movement of the masses, which can disorganise the state and render it powerless.

Divorced from the movement of the masses, the armed struggle cannot fulfill the role required by the socialist revolution. In 1905, the Bolsheviks formed armed units that carried out military actions, such as expropriations to finance the movement. In the course of the revolution, when the mass movement was at its high point, this was correct and necessary. But as soon as Lenin saw that the revolutionary movement was ebbing, he called for an end to the expropriations and a halt to guerrilla actions.

The reason for this is clear. The armed struggle, from the standpoint of the proletarian revolution, must be an integral part of the mass movement of the working class, and strictly subordinated to the leadership of the workers' party. As long as the mass movement is in action, there is little danger that the armed groups will degenerate. But when the movement ebbs, that can change. The armed wing attracts many of the most militant and self-sacrificing elements. But is can also attract other types: adventurers, lumpen proletarians and even common criminals. Without the firm guiding hand of the party, and without the control of the masses, such organisations can degenerate into simple criminal outfits. This has been seen many times in the history of the movement, and in many different countries, not least in Ireland.

The question must be posed concretely. How, for example, do we deal with the sectarian madmen who terrorise and murder innocent people? How do we deal with the criminal elements who all too often shelter behind the façade of paramilitary organisations? How do we protect our communities, when no trust can be placed in the police? Only by the establishment of a workers' militia, based on the unions, with cells in every factory and housing estate and close links with the community - that is to say, a militia on the lines of the ICA. The first duty of the militia is to defend the working people against criminals and sectarians. But this defensive function is a concrete way of preparing the proletariat for offensive actions against Capital at a later date, if and when conditions demand it.

The advocates of the armed struggle in Ireland over the last few decades showed that they did not have the least understanding of what a real armed struggle involves. Sure, they had all the necessary technical skills to cause mayhem. At the same time there were different tendencies involved with different perspectives for the struggle. But they lacked the understanding that would have permitted them to achieve their goals. In the end they failed totally. The conclusion is obvious: *The military wing of the movement must always be under the strict control of the political wing. Where this has not been the case, the most negative consequences have been seen.* This is exactly the conclusion outlined by Ta Power in his document on the history of the Irish Republican Socialist movement.

In the Russian Revolution of October 1917, nine-tenths of the task of the armed insurrection were accomplished in the months before the uprising. *These were not military tasks, but political ones*: patient and systematic work among the masses, in the army, in the factories, in the trade unions and in the soviets (workers' councils) to win over the working class to the side of the revolutionaries. Lenin's slogan at this time (from March to November) was not "armed struggle" but *"patiently explain!"* That is not a bad slogan for Republicans today! *Our task is not to win power but to win the masses.*

Marx explained long ago that ideas become a material force when they grip the minds of the masses. This is shown by the history of every revolution. The first aim of the revolution is therefore to *win the masses*. This is, in the first case, not a military but a political task. Before we can conquer power, we must first of all conquer the masses. Without a prolonged preliminary period of agitation, propaganda and organisation, there can be no question of a successful military struggle against the state. Any attempt to defeat the state by means of "single combat" will inevitably end in defeat and the disorganisation and demoralisation of the revolutionary forces. The experience of the past 30 years in Ireland amply confirms this prognosis.

Of course, we understand that, in the final analysis, the decisive questions are resolved by armed struggle. No devil has ever cut off its own claws! But in order to be successful, it must be an armed uprising of the masses, and not the activities of an armed elite operating outside the masses, and without any reference to them. The way to prepare for mass revolutionary action is by teaching the masses to have confidence in themselves. That was precisely what was achieved by the movement around the hunger strikes. This is what educates the masses in a revolutionary direction. The other tactic merely educates the masses backwards. It teaches them to trust in heroes and saviours, but not in themselves.

Guerrilla war is the classical mode of struggle, not of the proletariat, but of the peasantry. It makes some sense in a backward agrarian society such as Ireland was in the days of the Fenians, or China where there were peasant wars for several thousand years. There also the revolution took the form of a peasant war. In tsarist Russia, where the proletariat only numbered four million out of a total population of 150 million, and the peasantry was the overwhelming majority, the Bolsheviks nevertheless based themselves on the working class. True, they also made use of guerrilla war, but only as an auxiliary to the movement of the working class in the towns. Lenin supported guerrilla warfare in this sense in Russia in 1905, but as soon as the mass movement in the towns entered into decline after the defeat of the Moscow insurrection, he called a halt to the guerrilla tactics.

"Urban Guerrillaism"

However, the tactic of guerrilla war makes no sense at all in a developed capitalist country such as Ireland today, where the overwhelming majority of the population lives in towns. The so-called tactic of "urban guerrillaism" is only individual terrorism under a different name. In such a society, none of the conditions for waging a successful guerrilla struggle exist - and least of all in the North of Ireland. What is involved here is not the armed movement of the masses, but an armed elite which, while speaking in the name of the masses, operates behind the backs of the masses and without reference to them. The problem with this is that it does nothing to raise the revolutionary self-consciousness of the masses or their confidence in themselves.

The idea is cultivated that the masses must look for their salvation to a group of people who will somehow "save" them from their oppressors. It is clear that such tactics - even if they were to succeed - can never lead to a regime of workers' democracy. In the best variant, they would lead to the establishment of a regime where power would be in the hands of the elite that waged the struggle and would demand the fruits of their sacrifices. The masses would remain as passive cheerleaders. *Once again the masses would find themselves excluded from power and victims of a new form of oppression.*

In practice, however, even such a variant is ruled out. This type of armed struggle could never succeed in its objectives. And it has *not* succeeded. The British state, which they were supposed to be fighting against, has not been defeated, or even weakened. On the contrary, it is stronger than ever, armed and equipped with a battery of new weapons, anti-terrorist laws, reserve powers of all kinds, an army of spies and informers. Over thirty years they have perfected their methods of struggle against us and in the meantime brutalized a generation of British soldiers and accustomed British public opinion to all kinds of anti-democratic measures which in the past would have met with serious opposition. If the London government has partially scaled down the military presence in Northern Ireland, it has not been because they have been defeated but because they feel more confident - rightly or wrongly - that the situation is under control.

Connolly explained that the degree of violence required to settle accounts with the old ruling class depends on the concrete situation and the balance of class forces, which cannot be established a priori. But as a general rule we can say that the degree of violence that is required is in inverse proportion to the degree of support which the revolutionaries have built up among the masses. A colossal amount of power lies in the hands of the working class in modern society. Without the kind permission of the workers, not a light bulb shines, not a wheel turns, not a telephone rings. This is a formidable power, once it is organised and directed to the socialist transformation of society.

The problem is that the working class does not realise that it holds such power. It is the task of the revolutionary party to build up the confidence of the proletariat in its own power, and to convince it that it must use this power to effect a fundamental change in society, that, consequently, it does not require the services of saviours who will generously hand power to them on a silver platter - whether these "saviours" act from the ministerial bench or with bombs in their hands.

What conclusions should be drawn?

The dialectic of individual terrorism is always to achieve the opposite of what was intended. In the days of the Fenians, Marx warned that they could not expect the British workers to accept bombings directed at themselves. Actions such as the Birmingham pub bombings led to a wave of anti-Irish feeling in Britain, which did not help but hindered the national liberation struggle. On the other hand, the strengthening of the state and the stepping-up of repression constitute a threat and a danger to the labour movement, north and south of the border and in Britain also.

The first principle is to fight for *the unity of the working class*. In Ireland, we saw how Connolly and Larkin consistently fought to unite the workers and succeeded in bridging the sectarian divide. The argument that it is not possible to unite Protestant and Catholic workers in common struggle is wrong. At every key moment, there was a tendency of the workers to unite in struggle, as we have pointed out. The imperialists and capitalists strove to destroy this unity: *that is the root of the problem we face today*.

At every decisive turn, the possibility existed for developing a mass movement of the working people that could have cut across sectarianism. This was shown by Larkin and Connolly in 1911-14. It was again revealed in the unemployment struggles of the 1930s. In 1968-9, there was a spontaneous movement by the workers and shop stewards of Harland and Wolffs to set up committees to keep sectarian violence out of the shipyards. Unfortunately, there was no leadership of the calibre of Larkin and Connolly to give an organised and conscious expression to these strivings, and the opportunities were thrown away one by one with the most tragic results.

During the Hunger Strikes there was a mass movement of at least 100,000 people. With correct leadership this could have developed into a mass revolutionary movement against imperialism. But the Provisional leadership had no interest in promoting such a movement. They even opposed the proposal of the socialist Republicans to broaden the movement to include the trade unions, preferring to limit it to those elements that supported the "armed struggle". Once again, the opportunity was thrown away.

The labour movement, North and South, holds the key to the future. There was always a Labour tradition in the North. The Northern Ireland Labour Party (NILP) got 26 percent of the votes in 1962. As late as 1970 it still got 100,000 votes. But after decades of reformist degeneration, the NILP ended up as a tool of Orange sectarianism. This ruled it out as a political option for many workers. As a result, many workers from a Catholic background supported the SDLP, although this middle class moderate nationalist party was "Labour" in name only. The division of the Labour vote on sectarian lines hastened the demise of the NILP. After all, if one requires a sectarian party, why bother with a poor imitation, when one can have the genuine article?

The prior condition for success is the creation of a party based on the working class. Connolly and Larkin fought all their lives to build the Irish Labour Party. We have to win back this position in open struggle with the middle class nationalists. A vital task is the setting up of a Party of Labour based on the trade unions. The working class must re-establish its own independent voice, absent for so long. The trade unions, despite everything, remain united, solid and undefeated. Despite the disastrous policies of the union bureaucracy, this remains the case, and gives the only hope for future betterment. The recent strikes in the Republic, and the shift to the left in the unions in Britain opens up the prospect of a renewal of the class struggle that can cut across the deadly morass of sectarianism and prepare the ground for a new stage in the struggle.

We saw a magnificent display of class unity in the shape of the 18th January 2003 general strike against sectarianism, following the murder of postal worker Daniel McColgan by the loyalist thugs of the UFF. Unfortunately the trade union leaders failed to build on this unity. But the potential for united struggles on the part of the working class was clear for all to see.

The only cause worth fighting for is the struggle for the emancipation of the working class. In turn, the working class must inscribe on its banner the fight against all forms of oppression, including national oppression. "The border must be abolished!" Yes, of course! But the question is how? The old methods have failed to do this. It can only be achieved as a by-product of the socialist revolution. The question of the border can only be solved by the working class North and South conquering political power. Then it will be swept aside, as a man sweeps aside an irritating insect. *The border question can only be solved by the working class as a by-product of the socialist revolution. That is the lesson of the last hundred years of the national liberation struggle in Ireland and particularly the last thirty years.*

The first condition for a successful struggle against British imperialism is to unite the working class in the North, and to cut the ground from under sectarianism, which constitutes the main weapon in the imperialists' armoury. But this can never be achieved by the tactic of individual terrorism, which merely serves to drive the Unionist community into the arms of the British state and even to bolster Loyalism. If we have not learned that lesson from the past 30 years, we have learned nothing at all.

For those who imagine that the solution of all our problems lie in the elimination of the border, this will be seen at best as an irrelevance, at worse as a harmful diversion. For those of us who understand that the abolition of the border, though highly desirable and progressive - on a capitalist basis, even if it were possible, would solve precisely nothing, and that the only real solution is *workers' power*, it is a matter of life and death. The issue of the border cannot be separated from the revolutionary struggle against capitalism.

The petty bourgeoisie is an unstable class that always tends to swerve between the bourgeoisie and the proletariat. Its hallmark is extreme volatility. In critical situations, it tends to develop extreme and fanatical responses. Fascism and fundamentalism are examples of this. Extreme chauvinism is often a feature of petty bourgeois movements. The proletariat moves in an entirely different way. Its basic instinct is for *class unity* and tolerance. We must base ourselves on this healthy class instinct.

Class unity

The re-establishment of an independent movement of the working class and of class unity are the prior conditions for the creation of a militant anti-capitalist and anti-imperialist movement in the North and South of Ireland. As a first step, an energetic campaign should be launched for the setting up of a real Party of Labour, based on the trade unions. The programme of this Party must be democratically determined by the workers themselves, but it will clearly take its as its starting point the burning problems that affect all sections of the class in the North, which have for too long been pushed into the background. The questions which affect workers of all backgrounds, housing, health, education, if they are addressed from a class point of view, can expose the establishment parties of all shades who all support PFI, privatisation, and anti-working class policies to one extent or another.

For 80 years Labour has been told that it must wait. It has waited long enough. The argument that all the burning problems of working people must be put to one side until the issue of the border is solved can no longer be accepted. Moreover, the idea that a united Ireland will solve all our problems is false to the core. A united Ireland on a capitalist basis will solve absolutely nothing. We must address the immediate problems that face workers - both Catholics and Protestants - the lack of jobs and decent housing, wages and pensions, schools and hospitals.

While the southern economy has experienced something of a boom in the last period, in the North unemployment has risen. The traditional industries of shipbuilding and textiles had all but died, or were moved to developing nations in Asia. While there were attempts to bring in new investment, nothing major took hold. The DeLorean scandal was one of many cases of exploitation by multinationals of the conflict in the North for profit. The North didn't get the massive high-tech development the South did, so it has yet to feel the effects of the changes in production being felt elsewhere in the world.

In addition, the working class must fight for all democratic demands: free speech, the abolition of all anti-terrorist and anti-trade union legislation, full civil rights for prisoners, etc. This is part of our struggle, which we cannot renounce. But we will fight on these and every other issue, *with our own methods and our own class demands*. The unity of the working class in the North of Ireland can only brought about by the pursuit of class politics. Nothing else will do. A programme based on issues that can unite the class: jobs, wages, conditions, housing, women's rights - only the struggle for this can succeed where all else has failed. This is the way to prepare the ground for the ultimate aim: the revolutionary overthrow of capitalism in Ireland - North and South of the border - and in Britain, and on a European and world scale.

Part Thirteen

Against Sectarianism! For class unity!

There is an old story that after the battle of the Boyne, the boatman who was ferrying King William across the river Boyne asked him who had won the battle, to which the King replied: "It matters not to you, because you will still be the boatman."

In his lifetime, Connolly always fought for the unity of the working class above all national and religious lines. By concentrating on class issues, he succeeded in uniting the Catholic and Protestant workers in the struggle against their common enemy - the employing class. That is the only way to get out of the present mess. The only way to solve what remains of Ireland's national problem is as a by-product of the revolutionary struggle for socialism. That was true in Connolly's day. He had the vision and understanding to see this a hundred years ago. Today it is a hundred times more evident. There can be no reunification of Ireland while the working class remains divided along sectarian lines. Connolly's application of the ideas of Marxism to Ireland a century ago and the history of Ireland led him to the understand the leading role of the working class in the coming revolution, to understand the inability of the bourgeoisie to play any progressive role, and the socialist tasks of the revolution, completing the national democratic tasks in passing, as well as the need for the revolution to spread beyond our own borders.

The policies pursued by the middle-class Republican leaders over the past three decades have utterly failed in their goals. On the other hand, the methods they used have played havoc with the unity of the working class. True, the division between Catholics and Protestants has existed for a long time, encouraged by the deliberate actions of British imperialists, who early recognised that the splitting of the population of Northern Ireland on religious lines represented the surest means of strengthening their grip on Ireland. But this gulf has now been turned into a yawning abysm of bitterness and mutual mistrust. This means that the prospect of Irish unification is further off today than at any time in history. The only way in which we can begin to repair the damage is by fighting on a *class* programme, one that can unite the workers of both communities in struggle against their common enemy - the employing class.

The Role of religion

Religion has played a most negative role in Irish history. It has enabled the ruling class and imperialism to divide and fatally weaken the working class and the oppressed masses. Of course, men and women ought to be free to believe in any religion - or in none - without being molested by the state or suffering social or economic discrimination. Socialists will fight against discrimination in all its forms.

It is self-evident to anyone with the slightest knowledge of history that the Roman Catholic Church has never been a true friend of the national liberation struggle of the Irish people. It was a Pope who first handed Ireland to the English. It was another Pope who backed William of Orange against the Irish Catholics. The Catholic Church did nothing to protect the Irish language and culture when it was threatened with extinction. It opposed the United Irishmen and the Fenians and it destroyed Parnell. Above all, the Church bitterly opposed every advance of the labour movement in the early days. It denounced and persecuted Republicans, especially socialist Republicans.

The Church in the South has played a most reactionary role right up to the present. The bishops have been involved in most of the campaigns against social reform in Ireland, however, they themselves have been plagued by scandal, most notably the Bishop Casey affair, a bishop who had a son by an American woman, which the Church kept quiet for 18 years. Although divorce is now available in Ireland, it is a long and tortuous process. Statistics show that every year, several thousand Irish women travel to England to terminate pregnancies. Legally, children born out of wedlock suffer from the "stigma" of illegitimacy. Divorce, like abortion, brought forth major campaigns for reform. The youth and women of Ireland are in open revolt against the backward and reactionary legislation backed for generations by the Church.

Things are no better with Protestantism. For generations the Orange Order has been used as a mechanism used by the wealthy and powerful to control the Protestant masses and split the working class. The Orange Order has been used to perpetuate the sectarian make up of the Northern state. Every single head of the Six Counties has also been a senior member of the Orange Order. The poison of religious sectarianism and bigotry, the bad leftovers of the past, are the weapons whereby the ruling class perpetuates the divisions in the working class. In order to prevent Protestant workers identifying with their Catholic neighbours, the Order peddled the idea of an anti-Catholic society, led by the wealthy Protestants that offered all Protestants a place in its ranks, and the promise of promotion and privilege. The Orange parades were designed to allow the working class Protestant members a day in the sun to mix with their "betters" and at the same time lord it over their Catholic neighbours.

But this was a lie. The Protestant working class has nothing in common with the Protestant bankers, landlords and capitalists. Sectarianism was, and is, only a way of keeping the workers weak and divided. Radical Protestant workers to accusations of being "traitors" for refusing to support Orange bigotry. Connolly understood this very well. He and Larkin succeeded in uniting the Protestant and Catholic workers in struggle under difficult conditions by concentrating on the class questions. By skilful tactics they succeeded in splitting the Protestant workers away from the bosses. That is the correct way - the only way.

It is quite possible to achieve unity in struggle between the workers of both communities. Although unemployment is traditionally higher in Republican areas, there are plenty of unemployed Loyalists. There is plenty of bad housing in their areas, and they are also concerned about low wages and pensions. On social questions also there is a lot of discontent. Divorce is frowned upon by the Protestant churches, as is abortion, which is available only in limited cases. In the North's Protestant community, there are progressive people who would like to see social legislation there changed.

Not only the gun but also religion must be taken out of politics. People have the right to follow their religious beliefs. But that must not mean that one religion should dominate over another. True democrats demand the most radical separation of church and state. There can be no place for religion in the schools, where it fosters and perpetuates the division between Catholics and Protestants from childhood. Education must be secular, rational and scientific. If people want a religious education they must organise it outside school hours and pay for it themselves. Not a penny of taxpayers' money must be spent on religion. The money raised in taxes is the common property of all, irrespective of religious affiliation.

Sectarian divisions

It is time to put an end to the sectarian divisions that has bedevilled the working class of the North of Ireland for so long. Chief among the aims of the proletariat is that of upholding *the sacred unity of the working class*. Unity between the proletarians is the most important weapon they possess in their struggle against

Capital. Therefore, anything that tends to sow disunion among the workers is thoroughly reactionary and must be rejected. We stand for the unity of *all* workers, irrespective of race, nationality, language or religion. In the case of the Six Counties we stand for the *class unity* of Catholic and Protestant workers. Without this, no way forward is possible.

The constitution of Ireland must be changed as a prior condition for reunification, not only to appease the Protestants of the North, but because many in the Catholic community of both the North and South are also demanding changes on social issues. Many people on both sides of the sectarian divide feel that the present situation is intolerable and must be changed. We must base ourselves on this and fight on issues that unite working people, not those that divide us.

The so-called Accord has not abolished sectarianism but made it worse. The levels of sectarian violence tend to increase, while living standards and jobs are eroded. Sectarian madmen threaten workers' lives and make peoples' lives a misery. The politicians make fine speeches but have no solution to these problems. The fate of Yugoslavia constitutes a terrible warning of where a false policy on the national problem can lead. Along this road no progress is possible. *It is time to call a halt! We must strike out in a new direction - one that avoids the pitfalls of the past and opens the road to a successful struggle against capitalism and imperialism.*

The answer was shown by the magnificent general strike of the workers of the Six Counties against sectarianism on 18th January 2003. This shows the way forward! The working class will fight national oppression, but it will do so under its own banner, with its own policies and its own methods.

We will, of course, be accused of utopianism by those "realists" whose "practical" methods have landed us in the present mess. We are not worried about this accusation. It is not new. In his lifetime, Connolly was frequently accused of utopianism by his reactionary opponents, whose "realism" was just another way of expressing their slavish acceptance of the status quo. These cowardly servants of capitalism poured scorn on Connolly just like their descendents today. We will treat them with the same well-merited contempt with which Connolly did.

In the programme of socialism there is not a single atom of utopianism. Utopia signifies something that is impossible, something which is at variance with reality and that therefore cannot be. But in reality it is capitalism that is at variance with reality. The present economic crisis, during which every day thousands of workers are being thrown out of work, and the big companies close down factories as if they were so many matchboxes, shows that this is so.

If we look seriously at the problem of sectarianism we will see that, although it has its roots in history, it is perpetuated by the economic crisis and the limitations of the capitalist system. As long as there are not sufficient jobs and houses for everybody, there will always be the suspicion among the people of one community that they are unemployed or homeless because the others have taken their jobs and houses. A serious struggle against sectarianism therefore presupposes a serious struggle against capitalism.

Why is there a crisis? Because there are too many cars, too many computers, too much steel, too many microchips. In other words, it is a crisis of overproduction. Why is there overproduction? Only because capitalism has developed the productive forces to a point that they come into conflict with the narrow limits of the profits system. The main barriers to the further development of the productive forces are: the private ownership of the means of production and the nation state. This contradiction can only be removed by the elimination of both.

Nationalism and internationalism

Already in the pages of the *Communist Manifesto*, Marx and Engels pointed out that the socialist revolution, while national in form, is internationalist in content. Internationalism is a fundamental feature of scientific socialism.

The founders of scientific socialism argued that "the working men have no country." They insisted that:

"*1) In the national struggles of the proletarians of the different countries, they [the Communists] point out and bring to the front the common interests of the entire proletariat, independently of nationality.*" (Marx and Engels, Selected Works, vol, 1. p, 120, our emphasis.)

These profound words are even truer today than when they were first written.

Does this mean that we must ignore the national question, the oppression of women and other such questions? Of course not! The proletariat and its party are duty-bound to fight against *all* forms of oppression, including national oppression. Only in this way can we assemble and unite the forces necessary to overthrow capitalism. But in contrast to bourgeois and petty bourgeois nationalists, we point out that national oppression is only one manifestation of the central oppression from which all other forms ultimately derive: the division of society into classes and the enslavement of the working class by the bourgeoisie.

The national democratic tasks, which remain unsolved to this day, can only achieved by a struggle against the national bourgeoisie. The whole history of the national liberation struggle in the 20th century shows the correctness of this. The achievement of formal independence on a capitalist basis has solved nothing. Over half a century after independence, countries like India and Pakistan are more dependent on imperialism than before. They are still plundered through the mechanism of the world market and debt.

We can never accept the subordination of the interests of the working class to the demands of the nationalist bourgeoisie and petty bourgeoisie. Indeed, the greatest misfortune of the Irish labour movement was that it accepted the idea that "Labour must wait." The result is that the working class - and the entire people of Ireland - have been waiting for the best part of a hundred years for their social, economic and national rights, which the bourgeoisie has signally failed to achieve.

The border is, of course, an abomination that must be removed. It is not, however, the task of socialists to erect new frontiers. Our aim is altogether different: our aim is to abolish *all* frontiers, not just the one that separates the South from the North. We stand for a socialist revolution in the North and South of Ireland, and also a socialist revolution in Britain and the rest of Europe. In fact, without this, an Irish Workers' Republic would be only an ephemeral episode, like the Paris Commune.

British imperialism

British imperialism is our enemy. But the working class of England, Scotland and Wales is a potential ally, whose support and solidarity we must carefully cultivate and develop. Our aim is the establishment of a 32-county Irish Workers' Republic, linked to a democratic Socialist Federation of England, Scotland and Wales, as part of the Socialist United States of Europe and a Socialist World Federation. Does that seem utopian? But the fact remains that the supposedly "realistic" policies that the other side have been pursuing for the past seventy-odd years have turned out to be the worst - and most reactionary - utopianism. They have failed utterly in their basic aims, and it is about time that this was honestly and squarely stated.

Socialism is internationalist or it is nothing. The Irish national liberation movement has always been part of the world revolutionary movement, as Connolly always insisted:

"Just as '98 was an Irish expression of the tendencies embodied in the first French Revolution, as '48 throbbed in sympathy with the democratic and social upheavals on the Continent of Europe and England, so Fenianism was a responsive throb in the Irish heart to those pulsations in the heart of the European working class which elsewhere produced the International Working Men's Association." (Connolly, op cit, p. 164)

Socialism in one country is impossible. The struggle for socialism is an international struggle because capitalism is an international system. We are not nationalists but revolutionary internationalists. During the First World War, Connolly pursued a consistent internationalist policy, although that was a very difficult thing to do. Later, the Russian Revolution acted as a powerful stimulus to the Irish national liberation movement. It led to the spread of Communist ideas inside the Republican movement. Finally, the Civil Rights Movement of 1968 was also a part of a general ferment throughout Europe, exemplified by the general strike in France and student demonstrations all over Europe and America.

Yes, the proletariat is duty bound to fight against national oppression. But it is not at all bound to follow the dictates of alien classes with other aims and interests. It is by no means bound to subordinate itself to bourgeois and petty bourgeois movements with their own aims and agenda. On the contrary, the proletariat is duty bound to uphold its class independence, to pursue *only* those aims which will further the struggle for its own emancipation, and to *refuse* to support any others.

Forward to Connolly!

Wolf Tone once talked about "a chapter of great opportunities lost, of popular confidence betrayed". These words accurately describe the history of Ireland over the past hundred years. Ireland today is once again at a crossroads. The world is much changed since the days of the Civil Rights Movement and Bloody Sunday. On the face of it the situation might seem hopeless. In the Nationalist areas of the North, there is a war-weariness amongst the people. British troops have been in their communities since August 1969. An entire generation has been lost, burnt out, demoralised, killed. Yet, like the phoenix that rises from the ashes, the working class will always recover from even the greatest defeats. This is the only hope for Ireland and the world.

For the last 85 years, the Irish bourgeois nationalists have demonstrated their complete incapacity for solving the tasks of the Irish national liberation struggle. In 1922, the bourgeois leaders signed the partition of Ireland. This problem cannot be solved on a capitalist basis. The Irish bourgeoisie have had plenty of time to show what they can do, and they have failed.

Matters are no better with the petit bourgeois Republicans. For the last 30 years the Provisional IRA have been trying to solve the problem by a senseless campaign of bombing and shooting. These tactics of individual terrorism have absolutely nothing in common with the methods of Connolly and the Citizens Army, which were always based on class politics and organically linked to the proletariat and the mass workers organisations. A document of the IRSP stated correctly:

"As socialists, the IRSM believes that any settlement which does not answer the questions of national liberation and socialism cannot succeed, but will only put off the inevitable class struggle. The Irish Republican Socialist Movement is not frightened by this prospect; it will continue to organise as a revolutionary segment of the Irish working class, in the tradition of Connolly and Costello."

The socialist revolution in the North is inextricably linked to the perspective of socialist revolution in the South - and in Britain. In other words, it can only be solved with a proletarian and internationalist policy. There is still a ray of hope in the North of Ireland. Despite everything, the fundamental organisations of the working class - the trade unions - remain united. They are probably the only real non-sectarian mass organisations that still exist. This is the base upon which we can build! That would undoubtedly be the message of James Connolly, were he alive at this time.

So does this mean that we are proposing going back to the ideas and methods of the past? The subtitle of the present work refers to dialectics, and dialectics is concerned with progress, movement and development. We are revolutionaries and we therefore look forward to the future with optimism and hope. Nostalgia and longing for the past has no place in our outlook or philosophy. Yet dialectics teaches us that the process of development moves in a contradictory way. Old forms seem to recur constantly in history, and long-forgotten ideas can suddenly experience a rebirth. But on closer examination, this repetition is only apparent. There is always something new, an actual development, not an endless closed circle.

Scandalously, after Connolly's death the labour leaders in Ireland buried most of his works, while the bourgeois Nationalists consistently play down and distort his ideas and historical role. It is our duty to ensure that these marvellous writings get the widest possible circulation, especially among the younger generation. We believe the ideas of James Connolly were correct in all the fundamentals. That does not mean that we have to subscribe to every dot and comma. We do not have a religious attitude towards Connolly or anyone else. Today, more than eight decades since his death, certain details would have to be changed. But what is surprising is not how much of Connolly's thought needs to be revised. What is astonishing is how much remains completely valid.

Today, it is necessary to cut through all the fog of historical fantasy and nationalist mystification that surrounds the events of Easter Week, and see the key role of the proletariat. What a great opportunity was missed with the death of James Connolly! But the new generation must take the lesson to heart. Connolly failed because he did not create - as Lenin created - the necessary instrument with which to change society: a revolutionary party and a revolutionary leadership!

Today we pledge ourselves to defend the heritage of this great Marxist, fighter, and martyr of the working class. We must rescue the ideas of Connolly, which have been stolen and distorted beyond recognition by people who have nothing to do with Connolly, socialism or the working class. We must continue the fight for Connolly's ideas - the only ideas that can guarantee the ultimate victory. We must create the necessary revolutionary organisation, soundly based on the programme, policy and methods of Marxism. And we must understand that such an organisation must be firmly based in the only soil in which it can grow and flourish: the trade unions and the mass organisations of labour in Ireland, North and South, as well as on the other side of the Irish Sea.

A fighting working class movement is needed in Ireland, in Britain and internationally. Republican socialists have a vital role in the creation of such a movement. We view the working class as the only class that can provide and ensure that the movement of the future isn't based on failed slogans and strategies but in the direction of independent working class liberation, using whatever means are appropriate.

Hegel once wrote about an idea, which, having run the whole course of its development finally returns to the starting point. But it does so, enriched by all the wealth of content of its experience. Today, after three generations of struggle, we are in a position to appreciate just how right the great man was. We can appreciate him much more now than was possible during his lifetime. *James Connolly is the most modern of thinkers.*

Having experienced in our own flesh the bitterness of defeat, having seen so many brave fighters killed and imprisoned, with no appreciable result, we can finally understand that, when the Republican movement abandoned the road of James Connolly - the road of the class struggle and the socialist revolution, it took a fatally wrong turning. All mistakes must be paid for, and the movement has paid a very heavy price for its mistakes.

Today every honest Irish Republican will say: We owe it to the martyred dead, we owe it to ourselves, above all, we owe it to the future generations of Irish youth, to recognise our errors and firmly retrace our steps. In so doing we must finally decide to take the route mapped out by the leader of the Easter Rising: *the road that unites the working class, not the one that divides it: the road of socialist revolution.*

Marx pointed out the most elementary truth: *that the emancipation of the working class is the task of the working class, and only the working class.* The Easter Rising was a glorious harbinger of what is still to come. The job was left unfinished in 1916. The task now falls upon the shoulders of the new generation of workers and youth. Armed with the ideas of Marxism, the ideas of Connolly, the ultimate victory is guaranteed. We echo the confidence in the Irish working class and the revolutionary optimism expressed by James Connolly when he wrote in 1914:

"Ireland may yet set the torch to a European conflagration, that will not burn out until the last throne and the last capitalist bond and debenture will be shrivelled on the funeral pyre of the last war-lord."

Other titles from Wellred

▶ **In the Cause of Labour - History of British Trade Unionism**
By Rob Sewell
Price: £ 14.99

Pub. Date: 2003
Format: Paperback
No. Pages: 480
ISBN: 1900007142

History of British Trotskyism ◀
By Ted Grant
Price: £ 9.99

Pub. Date: 2002
Format: Paperback
No. Pages: 310
ISBN: 190000710X

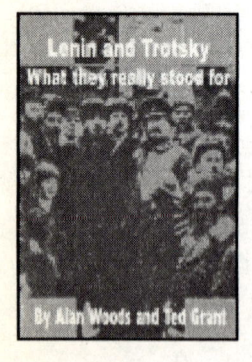

▶ **Lenin and Trotsky - What they really stood for**
By Alan Woods and Ted Grant
Price: £ 8.95

Pub. Date: 2000
Format: Paperback
No. Pages: 221
ISBN: 8492183268

Bolshevism - The Road to Revolution ◀
By Alan Woods
Price: £ 15.00
Pub. Date: 1999
Format: Paperback
No. Pages: 636
ISBN: 1900007053